THE FRONTIER THESIS

THE FRONTIER THESIS

Valid Interpretation of American History?

Edited by RAY ALLEN BILLINGTON

Henry E. Huntington Library and Art Gallery

KRIEGER PUBLISHING COMPANY
MALABAR, FLORIDA

"The Atlantic frontier was compounded of fisherman, fur-trader, miner, cattle-raiser, and farmer. Excepting the fisherman, each type of industry was on the march toward the West, impelled by an irresistible attraction.Each passed in successive waves across the continent. Stand at Cumberland Gap and watch the procession of civilization, marching single file-- the buffalo following the trail to the salt springs, the Indian, the fur-trader and hunter, the cattle-raiser, the pioneer farmer--and the frontier has passed by."--Frederick Jackson Turner

Original Edition 1966
Reprint Edition 1977

Printed and Published by
ROBERT E. KRIEGER PUBLISHING COMPANY, INC.
KRIEGER DRIVE
MALABAR, FLORIDA 32950

Copyright©1966 by
HOLT, RINEHART AND WINSTON, INC.
Reprinted by Arrangement

Library of Congress Cataloging-in-Publication Data
Billington, Ray Allen, 1903-   ed.
  The frontier thesis.

  Reprint of the ed. published by Holt, Rinehart and
Winston, New York, in series: American problem studies.
  Bibliography: p.
  1. Turner, Frederick Jackson, 1861-1932. The frontier
in American history--Addresses, essays, lectures.
2. Frontier thesis--Addresses, essays, lectures. I. Title.
[E179.5.B625 1977]   973   77-9103
ISBN 0-88275-586-2

10   9   8   7   6   5   4

CONTENTS

Feb. 23, 1893

Pres. C. K. Adams,
    Univ. of Wis.,

Dear sir!

        I thank you for the invi-
tation to present a paper at the ensu-
ing meeting of the American Historical Association, and am glad to
accept. My subject will be "The
Significance of the Frontier in American History"

            Very truly yours

                Frederick J. Turner

INTRODUCTION

No interpretation of American history—not even the economic determinism popularized by Charles A. Beard—has attracted such loyal support or inspired such bitter criticism as the frontier thesis of Frederick Jackson Turner. Almost from the summer day in 1893, when Turner read his paper on "The Significance of the Frontier in American History" before a Chicago meeting of the American Historical Association, historians have defended or attacked his views with a vehemence usually associated with less tranquil professions. Even today the controversy continues and it will probably rage as long as the American people are interested in their past.

The hypothesis advanced by Turner in his 1893 paper and subsequent writings may be summarized briefly. The differences that distinguish the American people from Europeans, he argued, are due in part to the three-centuries-long period of expansion required to settle the continent. During this entire time men left their homes to begin life anew on successive frontiers, shedding some of their cultural baggage as they advanced. In their new homes more of the habits of civilization were discarded because many of the customs and institutions necessary in the thickly populated communities of the East were inappropriate in the thinly peopled hamlets or farm areas of the West. As fewer controls were needed governmental functions were simplified, economic activity reverted to self-sufficiency, social organization eroded away, and cultural activities slowed. On the successive frontiers, Turner believed, an atomization of society occurred, and with it a reversion toward primitivism.

Gradually, however, latecomers swelled the population of each pioneer settlement, and as their numbers increased so did the level of civilization. Governmental controls tightened, economic specialization began, the social organization grew more complex, and cultural activities multiplied. The mature social order that eventually evolved from each pioneer community differed noticeably from those of the eastern regions, from which its settlers came. These alterations, Turner believed, resulted from a variety of forces peculiar to the frontier environment. There men were few and land plentiful; this ratio provided a relatively greater opportunity for individual self-better-

1

ment than existed in long-settled areas. On the frontiers, men from different backgrounds met and mingled, each contributing traits and habits, which slightly altered the emerging civilization. There, too, social units were so divided that each followed a separate evolutionary course, with the deviations inevitable in such a situation. More simply, Turner believed that an "Americanization" of men and institutions took place.

The result was, in Hector St. John de Crèvecoeur's phrase, a "new man," who differed in discernible ways from his European cousins. His faith in democracy had been deepened by life in a land where equality of opportunity and absence of hereditary distinctions blurred traditional class lines. His nationalistic sentiments had been quickened by reliance on a central government, which alone could provide defense, roads, land sales, and other necessities. His sense of individual self-sufficiency had been intensified by an abundance of natural resources that freed men from dependence on social controls. These changes in basic attitudes, Turner felt, provided Americans with value systems that could have come only from the frontiering experience. He also believed that pioneering altered some behavioral patterns. The plentiful resources amid which men lived made them wasteful and scornful of conservation. Their isolated lives forced them to develop inventive skills and made them receptive to innovation. Their tendency to move readily in search of fresh opportunity lessened their attachment to place and converted the Americans into a nation of wanderers. The hard work essential in pioneering quickened their materialistic impulses and lessened their respect for abstract thinkers and for creativity in the arts. Turner recognized that these traits were not uniquely American, but he believed that they existed in exaggerated form among Americans because of the frontiering experience.

The immediate reception of Turner's paper was less than enthusiastic. To a generation of historians, believing with Edward A. Freeman that "history is past politics, and politics is present history," and loyal to the thesis of Herbert Baxter Adams that all American institutions had derived from their "germs" in the folkmoots of medieval Germany, a doctrine that stressed the differences rather than the similarities between Europeans and Americans, and that focused on individuals rather than governments, was too heretical to be immediately accepted. Edward Everett, to whom Turner sent a copy of his paper, acknowledged the receipt of "your curious and interesting" article, and Theodore Roosevelt wrote that he had "struck some first class ideas, and . . . put into definite shape a good deal of thought which has been floating around rather loosely." This was faint praise indeed for a thesis that was to revolutionize the study of American history.

But Turner was to have his due. Over the years he both popularized and expanded his hypothesis in a number of articles and lectures. These attracted increasing attention, both among a general public much concerned with the

West in a day when the balance of power was shifting toward the Pacific, and in a scholarly community questing for a workable value system at a time when industrialism and urbanization were altering national behavior. As historians came to accept his views, scholars in other disciplines awakened to the fact that the frontier experience must have altered every form of human behavior. Economists, political scientists, and geographers restudied the past to show the influence of pioneering on commercial growth, constitution-making, and settlement. Students of American letters produced volumes on the literature of the midwestern frontier and the frontier in American literature. If, as one critic, noted, the American Historical Association had by the 1920s been converted into "One Big Turner *Verein*," the other professional associations were not far behind.

This was unfortunate. Turner had made no extravagant claims for either the validity or inviolability of his frontier thesis. As an exacting scholar he was aware that he had advanced a hypothesis and nothing more; that hypothesis had to be tested before it could be applied to American history and other disciplines as well. His followers were less cautious; to them the thesis was the Divine Word, utterly unassailable. They saw the frontier not as *one* force helping to mold the American character but as *the* force, solely responsible for the behavior of the people and the only key needed to unlock the secrets of the nation's history. Between the early twentieth century and the close of the 1920s the frontier hypothesis was virtually unquestioned as the Holy Writ of American historiography.

A reaction against such unreasonable overemphasis was bound to come. This began at about the time of Turner's death in 1932 and was an outgrowth of the intellectual climate of the Depression decade. Younger historians, concerned with an economic cataclysm that threatened all civilization, rebelled against emphasis on a rural past when the problems that demanded solution stemmed from an urban present. They disliked Turner's emphasis on individualism at a time when collective action seemed essential to check the plunge into chaos; they disapproved of his stress on nationalism in an era when international cooperation was necessary to meet a world crisis. Turner's methodology was also suspect among young scholars, who saw his overglorification of a single casual force as unrealistic when every passing day demonstrated the complexity of human motivation. Marxists found him guilty of ignoring the class struggle and industrialization as being prime forces in shaping national behavior. The intellectual atmosphere of the 1930s, no less than the overmagnification of the frontier thesis by Turner's uncritical disciples, demanded a reexamination of the whole problem of causation in American history.

During the next two decades the critics of the hypothesis had their day, arguing that the frontier was not, and never had been, a major force in molding the American character. Their attack took two forms. One group focused on Turner's presentation of the hypothesis, finding in his lack of precise definitions, inexact phraseology, sweeping metaphors, tendency to exaggerate, proneness to draw broad conclusions from inadequate evidence, and his indifference to other casual forces, proof that the frontier thesis was not only suspect but positively wrong. How, they asked, could pioneering foster nationalism and sectionalism, individualism and cooperation, materialism and idealism, innovation and conformity, coarseness and optimism, all at the same time? How could a frontier environment, which persisted only briefly before the settlement process was completed, exert such an enduring influence over frontiersmen and the nation as a whole? To these critics, Turner's essays were so faulty that they felt the thesis itself had to be rejected.

The second group launched their barbs at aspects of the frontier hypothesis. Some first questioned, then rejected, what is known as the safety-valve doctrine—the belief that in periods of depression the frontier drained displaced workers westward, thus decreasing the labor supply and elevating the wages of those who remained. Others disputed Turner's supposed assertion that democracy originated in the forests of the West rather than in Europe. Still others showed that the frontier was an area where cooperative activity— in the form of cabin raisings, logrollings, husking bees, and similar activities —was more common than in Eastern villages; how, they asked, could such a region foster individualism? Some critics disputed Turner's emphasis on American nationalism and argued that the nation's civilization had been transplanted from Europe rather than originated in the West. Hardly a concept associated with Turner remained unquestioned during the two decades when this critical examination went on.

This period of rejection reached its climax in the late 1940s. Beginning in the 1950s the tide of historical judgment began to shift once more as the subject came to be considered by what has been called the third generation of the frontier hypothesis. Since that time historians to a degree, and students in other disciplines to an even greater degree, have shown an increasing willingness to examine the thesis objectively rather than to accept unquestioningly or reject completely as in the prior two generations. To these scholars Turner's *statement* of the thesis is unimportant; what is important to them is whether the thesis itself has validity. This can be determined only by extensive testing —using the variety of tools available to social scientists, with emphasis at the grass-roots level where statistical evidence can be employed. According to disciples of this third generation, many of the critics of the 1930s and 1940s were as extravagant in their claims, questionable in their methodology, and suspect in their findings as they accused Turner of being.

The selections in this volume have been arranged to reveal the extent of the differences between the second and third generations. It begins with two selections by Frederick Jackson Turner, which state the frontier thesis. The first indictment of. Turner's presentation of his thesis, and of the thesis itself, is by George W. Pierson. In the essay reproduced in part here and in later essays, Pierson emphasizes the inconsistencies and contradictions in Turner's writings, and the vagueness of the concept he was expostulating. Today's reader should keep in mind two questions: does Turner's presentation of the frontier hypothesis negate the validity of the hypothesis as Pierson suggests and was Turner more guilty of inexact definitions and unprecise semantics than other historians of his day—or of today? Consistency and precision are virtues rarely found in students who deal with the inconsistency of human behavior. Yet Pierson performed a valuable service by calling attention to the need for more exact language in dealing with a subject as complex as the frontier hypothesis.

Critics of the thesis entered the arena of controversy when they turned their attention from the form in which it was presented to the validity of its particular aspects. One phase concerned the operation of the frontier "safety valve." Turner probably did not subscribe as completely as most of his contemporaries to the belief that the West restrained radical agitation in the United States by draining excess wage earners from the East during depression eras. In his early writings he did refer to the "gate of escape to the free conditions of the frontier," and to the Mississippi Valley as opening "a refuge to the oppressed of all regions," but further study made him more cautious until he could write in his last book that "the opportunity of direct access to cheap Western lands was not open to the poorer people of the Northeastern states and of Europe." Yet the frontier thesis as understood by his contemporaries and disciples did postulate an operating safety valve, and its critics of the 1930s and 1940s were justified in reexamining the whole question.

This they did with telling results. The frontier, they argued, served neither as a "direct" safety valve (drawing off Eastern workers in times of depression), nor as an "indirect" safety valve (attracting displaced Eastern farmers who might otherwise have competed for jobs in factories). To prove this, they advanced statistical evidence showing that migration westward decreased in bad times and increased in good, that the cost of moving to the frontier was beyond the means of the nineteenth-century workman, and that population movements tended to swell city populations more rapidly than rural. In the most telling of the numerous examinations of the question, Fred A. Shannon voices the opinion that if a safety valve did exist, it operated by attracting excess farm workers to the cities and hence lessening agrarian discontent in the late nineteenth century.

During the 1960s economists counted among the third generation have raised serious questions concerning Shannon's findings and those of his contemporaries. Earlier critics, they feel, erred by focusing exclusively on the operation of a "direct" and "indirect" safety valve. To be effective in lessening wage-earner discontent, the frontier would have to elevate wages and decrease competition for jobs. To determine its role in this capacity, its effect on the entire economy must be appraised, both immediately and over the course of years as the sequential exploitation of frontier resources continues. Of the scholars holding to this line, none has presented a more effective argument than Ellen von Nardroff. Reviewing the evidence for and against the doctrine, she concludes that the frontier, operating as a "resources" safety valve and as a "socio-psychological" safety valve, did diminish worker discontent just as the Turnerians postulated.

As controversial as the critics' assault on the safety-valve doctrine was their attack during the 1930s and 1940s on Turner's contention that democracy was a product of the forest environment. This began in 1930 with the publication of an essay by Benjamin F. Wright, Jr., reproduced here. Wright in this and later publications charged the frontier school with two basic errors. Democracy, he insists, was well developed in England before the settlement of the colonies and was simply transplanted to them; if this was not so, how can we account for its failure to develop in New France and New Spain? Within the United States democratic gains had originated in the East rather than the West. It was in the East that crusades began for manhood suffrage, equitable representation, restrictions on executive authority, women's rights, and similar reforms. The frontier, argues Wright and those who echo his views, was imitative rather than creative in the sphere of government, following the lead of Eastern cities, where pressure from the working classes underlay the demand for change.

Recent students have answered these criticisms by arguing two propositions. Turner, they contend, had maintained that *American* democracy, not democracy in its broader sense, was fostered by the frontier environment. This point has been stressed by John D. Barnhart in his book, *Valley of Democracy,* a portion of which is reprinted in this volume. Secondly, they argue that this brand of democracy can be appraised only by detailed local studies of pioneer communities, where alterations in the social structure generated by the frontier experience strengthened faith in equality and belief in self-rule. In new settlements the necessity for local decision-making, lack of a prior leadership structure, relative unimportance of hereditary status distinctions, and leveling influence of the opportunity for self-improvement provided by cheap land, all operated to generate the democratic spirit in its most American sense. The most searching inquiry along these lines has been made by Merle Curti, who directed a grass-roots statistical study of one Western county during its pioneering era. The conclusions he reached are included in this collection of readings as he presented them in *The Making of an American Community.* They should be read with caution, as Curti himself suggests, for the sampling is too scant to justify broad conclusions. Yet his findings, and those of others who have based their results on less thorough examinations of the evidence, indicate that the frontier may have had some impact on the unique American brand of democracy.

If Turner's critics of the 1930s and 1940s challenged his assumptions on the frontier's role as a safety valve and breeder of democratic practices, recent scholars have asked even more searching questions concerning the nature and influence of the pioneering experience. Their queries have taken two forms. One group, represented in this book by Earl Pomeroy, has cautioned investigators to weigh the relative importance of environment and continuity on frontiersmen before leaping to any rash conclusions concerning the effect of Westward expansion on men or institutions. The traits and habits of civilization, they argue, have persisted amid most primitive conditions and have bulked larger than any others in shaping the American character. Members of this group, unlike earlier critics, have no basic quarrel with Turner's fundamental beliefs; they merely stress the complexity of forces shaping human behavior as would Turner himself.

A second group of modern scholars has advanced alternative explanations for the distinctive features of the American character and has felt called upon to dispute the frontier hypothesis in doing so. Some hold that these features are traceable to the migratory habits of the people of the United States; incessant moving about has accentuated their wastefulness, nationalism, and democracy. Others insist that the abundance made available by the sequential exploitation of nature's resources has made the Americans a "people of plenty," and that their behavioral patterns are a response to this relative wealth. Turnerians answer that these views, represented in this volume be the demographer Everett S. Lee, and the historian David M. Potter are not in conflict with their own; had there been no frontier, the Americans would have developed no migratory habits and would have been lacking the abundance needed to make them a people of plenty.

The arguments over particular features of the frontier thesis become meaningful only if they are combined to present a united case for or against its validity. For that reason this volume concludes with two summaries. The first, published in 1949 by Richard Hofstadter, mirrors opposition to the hypothesis at its high-water mark. It neatly summarizes the arguments employed by a score of attackers and adds Hofstadter's own penetrating insights. The second, written in 1957 by the British historian Harry C. Allen, maintains with wit and knowledge the validity of the thesis as reflected in more recent scholarship than that available to Hofstadter. Each presents a convincing case. The reader must decide the verdict.

Whatever your present decision, you may later wish to revise it in the light of new evidence. Far more research remains to be done, far more frontiers studied in depth, far more theories critically tested, before historians can assume that the validity of the frontier thesis has been proved or disproved. Today's students of the subject, unlike those of a generation ago, belive the hypothesis to be a useful tool and one essential to understanding the American character. They differ from the original Turnerians in knowing that it is only one of many tools and that any assumption that pioneering alone shaped American civilization is false. This is a judgment to which Frederick Jackson Turner would have subscribed for he, unlike some of his disciples, realized that man's behavior is too complex to be ascribed to any one influence.

In the reprinted selections footnotes appearing in the original sources have in general been omitted unless they contribute to the argument or better understanding of the selection.

When FREDERICK JACKSON TURNER (1861–1932) read his essay on "The Significance of the Frontier in American History" in 1893, he touched off a controversy that has stirred historians since that time and will continue to stir them for years to come. At that time Turner was a relatively young man. He had graduated from the University of Wisconsin in 1885, earned a Master of Arts degree from that institution in 1887, and completed work for the doctorate at the Johns Hopkins University in 1890. Returning to Wisconsin as assistant professor of history, he included the study of westward expansion in his new course on the economic and social history of the United States. The reading necessary to prepare that course suggested the bold interpretation of the American past that is printed in part below.*

Statement of the Frontier Thesis

In a recent bulletin of the Superintendent of the Census for 1890 appear these significant words: "Up to and including 1880 the country had a frontier of settlement, but at present the unsettled area has been so broken into by isolated bodies of settlement that there can hardly be said to be a frontier line. In the discussion of its extent, its westward movement etc., it can not, therefore, any longer have a place in the census reports." This brief official statement marks the closing of a great historic movement. Up to our own day American history has been in a large degree the history of the colonization of the Great West. The existence of an area of free land, its continuous recession, and the advance of American settlement westward, explain American development.

Behind institutions, behind constitutional forms and modifications, lie the vital forces that call these organs into life and shape them to meet changing conditions. The peculiarity of American institutions is, the fact that they have been compelled to adapt themselves to the changes of an expanding people—to the changes involved in crossing a continent, in winning a wilderness, and in developing at each area of this progress out of the primitive economic and political conditions of the frontier into the

* From Frederick Jackson Turner, "The Significance of the Frontier in American History," American Historical Association, *Annual Report for the Year 1893* (Washington, 1894), pp. 199–227.

complexity of city life. Said Calhoun in 1817, "We are great, and rapidly—I was about to say fearfully—growing!" So saying, he touched the distinguishing feature of American life. All peoples show development; the germ theory of politics has been sufficiently emphasized. In the case of most nations, however, the development has occurred in a limited area; and if the nation has expanded, it has met other growing peoples whom it has conquered. But in the case of the United States we have a different phenomenon. Limiting our attention to the Atlantic coast, we have the familiar phenomenon of the evolution of institutions in a limited area, such as the rise of representative government; the differentiation of simple colonial governments into complex organs; the progress from primitive industrial society, without division of labor, up to manufacturing civilization. But we have in addition to this a recurrence of the process of evolution in each western area reached in the process of expansion. Thus American development has exhibited not merely advance along a single line, but a return to primitive conditions on a continually advancing frontier line, and a new development for that area. American social development has been continually beginning over again on the frontier. This perennial rebirth, this fluidity of American life, this expansion westward with its new opportunities, its continuous touch with the simplicity of primitive society, furnish the forces dominating American character. The true point of view in the history of this nation is not the Atlantic coast, it is the Great West. Even the slavery struggle, which is made so exclusive an object of attention by writers like Professor von Holst, occupies its important place in American history because of its relation to westward expansion.

In this advance, the frontier is the outer edge of the wave—the meeting point between savagery and civilization. Much has been written about the frontier from the point of view of border warfare and the chase, but as a field for the serious study of the economist and the historian it has been neglected.

The American frontier is sharply distinguished from the European frontier —a fortified boundary line running through dense populations. The most significant thing about the American frontier is, that it lies at the hither edge of free land. In the census reports it is treated as the margin of that settlement which has a density of two or more to the square mile. The term is an elastic one, and for our purpose does not need sharp definition. We shall consider the whole frontier belt, including the Indian country and the outer margin of the "settled area" of the census reports. This paper will make no attempt to treat the subject exhaustively; its aim is simply to call attention to the frontier as a fertile field for investigation, and to suggest some of the problems which arise in connection with it.

In the settlement of America we have to observe how European life entered the continent, and how America modified and developed that life and reacted on Europe. Our early history is the study of European germs developing in an American environment. Too exclusive attention has been paid by institutional students to the Germanic origins, too little to the American factors. The frontier is the line of most rapid and effective Americanization. The wilderness masters the colonist. It finds him a European in dress, industries, tools, modes of travel, and thought. It takes him from the railroad car and puts him in the birch canoe. It strips off the garments of civilization and arrays him in the hunting shirt and the moccasin. It puts him in the log cabin of the Cherokee and Iroquois and runs an Indian palisade around him. Before long he has gone to planting Indian corn and plowing with a sharp stick; he shouts the war cry and takes the scalp in orthodox Indian fashion. In short, at the frontier the environment is at first too strong for the man. He must accept the conditions which it furnishes, or perish, and so he fits himself into the Indian clearings and follows the Indian trails. Little by little he transforms the wilderness, but the outcome is not the old Europe, not simply the development of Germanic germs, any more than the first phenomenon was a case of reversion to the Germanic mark. The fact is, that here is a new product that is American. At first, the frontier was the Atlantic coast. It was the frontier of Europe in a very real sense. Moving westward, the frontier became more and more American. As successive terminal moraines result from successive glaciations, so each frontier leaves its traces behind it, and when it becomes a settled area the region still partakes of the frontier characteristics. Thus the advance of the frontier has meant a steady movement away from the influence of Europe, a steady growth of independence on American lines. And to study this advance, the men who grew up under these conditions, and the political, economic, and social results of it, is to study the really American part of our history. . . .

Loria, the Italian economist, has urged the study of colonial life as an aid in understanding the stages of European development, affirming that colonial settlement is for economic science what the mountain is for geology, bringing to light primitive stratifications. "America," he says, "has the key to the historical enigma which Europe has sought for centuries in vain, and the land which has no history reveals luminously the course of universal history." There is much truth in this. The United States lies like a huge page in the history of society. Line by line as we read this continental page from West to East we find the record of social evolution. It begins with the Indian and the hunter; it goes on to tell of the disintegration of savagery by the entrance of the trader, the pathfinder of civilization; we read the annals of the pastoral stage in ranch life; the exploitation of the soil by the raising of unrotated crops of corn and wheat in sparsely settled farming communities; the intensive culture of the denser farm settlement; and finally the manufacturing organization with city and factory system. This page is familiar to the student of census statistics, but how little of it has been used by our historians. Particularly in eastern States this page is a palimpsest. What is now a manufacturing State was in an earlier decade an area of intensive farming. Earlier yet it had been a wheat area, and still earlier the "range" had attracted the cattleherder. Thus Wisconsin, now developing manufacture, is a State with varied agricultural interests. But earlier it was given over to almost exclusive grain-raising, like North Dakota at the present time.

Each of these areas has had an influence in our economic and political history; the evolution of each into a higher stage has worked political transformation. But what constitutional historian has made any adequate attempt to interpret political facts by the light of these social areas and changes? . . . .

We may next inquire what were the influences on the East and on the Old World. A rapid enumeration of some of the more noteworthy effects is all that I have time for.

First, we note that the frontier promoted the formation of a composite nationality for the American people. The coast was preponderantly English, but the later tides of continental immigration flowed across to the free lands. This was the case from the early colonial days. The Scotch-Irish and the Palatine Germans, or "Pennsylvania Dutch," furnished the dominant element in the stock of the colonial frontier. With these peoples were also the freed indented servants, or redemptioners, who at the expiration of their time of service passed to the frontier. Governor Spotswood of Virginia writes in 1717, "The inhabitants of our frontiers are composed generally of such as have been transported hither as servants, and, being out of their time, settle themselves where land is to be taken up and that will produce the necessarys of life with little labour." Very generally these redemptioners were of non-English stock. In the crucible of the frontier the immigrants were Americanized, liberated, and fused into a mixed race, English in neither nationality nor characteristics. The process has gone on from the early days to our own. Burke and other writers in the middle of the eighteenth century believed that Pennsylvania was "threatened with the danger of being wholly foreign in language, manners, and perhaps even inclinations." The German and Scotch-Irish elements in the frontier of the South were only less great.

In the middle of the present century the German element in Wisconsin was already so considerable that leading publicists looked to the creation of a German state out of the commonwealth by concentrating their colonization. Such examples teach us to beware of misinterpreting the fact that there is a common English speech in America into a belief that the stock is also English.

In another way the advance of the frontier decreased our dependence on England. The coast, particularly of the South, lacked diversified industries, and was dependent on England for the bulk of its supplies. In the South there was even a dependence on the Northern colonies for articles of food. Governor Glenn, of South Carolina, writes in the middle of the eighteenth century: "Our trade with New York and Philadelphia was of the sort, draining us of all the little money and bills we could gather from other places for their bread, flour, beer, hams, bacon, and other things of their produce, all which, except beer, our new townships begin to supply us with, which are settled with very industrious and thriving Germans. This no doubt diminishes the number of shipping and the appearance of our trade, but it is far from being a detriment to us." Before long the frontier created a demand for merchants. As it retreated from the coast it became less and less possible for England to bring her supplies directly to the consumer's wharfs, and carry away staple crops, and staple crops began to give way to diversified agriculture for a time. The effect of this phase of the frontier action upon the northern section is perceived when we realize how the advance of the frontier aroused seaboard cities like Boston, New York, and Baltimore, to engage in rivalry for what Washington called "the extensive and valuable trade of a rising empire."

The legislation which most developed the powers of the national government, and played the largest part in its activity, was conditioned on the frontier. Writers have discussed the subjects of tariff, land, and internal improvement, as subsidiary to the slavery question. But when American history comes to be rightly viewed it will be seen that the slavery question is an incident. In the period from the end of the first half of the present century to the close of the Civil War slavery rose to primary, but far from exclusive, importance. But this does not justify Dr. von Holst (to take an example) in treating our constitutional history in its formative period down to 1828 in a single volume, giving six volumes chiefly to the history of slavery from 1828 to 1861, under the title "Constitutional History of the United States." The growth of nationalism and the evolution of American political institutions were dependent on the advance of the frontier. Even so recent a writer as Rhodes, in his "History of the United States since the Compromise of 1850," has treated the legislation called out by the western advance as incidental to the slavery struggle.

This is a wrong perspective. The pioneer needed the goods of the coast, and so the grand series of internal improvement and railroad legislation began, with potent nationalizing effects. Over internal improvements occurred great debates, in which grave constitutional questions were discussed. Sectional groupings appear in the votes, profoundly significant for the historian. Loose construction increased as the nation marched westward. But the West was not content with bringing the farm to the factory. Under the lead of Clay— "Harry of the West"—protective tariffs were passed, with the cry of bringing the factory to the farm. The disposition of the public lands was a third important subject of national legislation influenced by the frontier.

The public domain has been a force of profound importance in the nationalization and development of the government. The effects of the struggle of the landed and the landless States, and of the Ordinance of 1787, need no discussion. Administratively the frontier called out some of the highest and most vitalizing activities of the general government. The purchase of Louisiana was perhaps the constitutional turning point in the history of the Republic, inasmuch as it afforded both a new area for national legislation and the occasion of the downfall of the policy of strict construction. But the purchase of Louisiana was called out by frontier needs and demands. As frontier States accrued to the Union the national power grew. In a speech on the dedication of the Calhoun monument Mr. Lamar explained: "In 1789 the States were the creators of the Federal Government; in 1861 the Federal Government was the creator of a large majority of the States."

When we consider the public domain from the point of view of the sale and disposal of the public lands we are again brought face to face with the frontier. The policy of the United States in dealing with its lands is in sharp contrast with the European system of scientific administration. Efforts to make this domain a source of revenue, and to withhold it from emigrants in order that settlement might be compact, were in vain. The jealousy and the fears of the

East were powerless in the face of the demands of the frontiersmen. John Quincy Adams was obliged to confess: "My own system of administration, which was to make the national domain the inexhaustible fund for progressive and unceasing internal improvement, has failed." The reason is obvious; a system of administration was not what the West demanded; it wanted land. Adams states the situation as follows: "The slaveholders of the South have bought the cooperation of the western country by the bribe of the western lands, abandoning to the new Western States their own proportion of the public property and aiding them in the design of grasping all the lands into their own hands. Thomas H. Benton was the author of this system, which he brought forward as a substitute for the American system of Mr. Clay, and to supplant him as the leading statesman of the West. Mr. Clay, by his tariff compromise with Mr. Calhoun, abandoned his own American system. At the same time he brought forward a plan for distributing among all the States of the Union the proceeds of sales of the public lands. His bill for that purpose passed both Houses of Congress, but was vetoed by President Jackson, who, in his annual message of December, 1832, formally recommended that all public lands should be gratuitously given away to individual adventurers and to the States in which the lands are situated."

"No subject," said Henry Clay, "which has presented itself to the present, or perhaps any preceding, Congress, is of greater magnitude than that of the public lands." When we consider the far-reaching effects of the government's land policy upon political, economic, and social aspects of American life, we are disposed to agree with him. But this legislation was framed under frontier influences, and under the lead of Western statesmen like Benton and Jackson. Said Senator Scott of Indiana in 1841: "I consider the preëmption law merely declaratory of the custom or common law of the settlers."

It is safe to say that the legislation with regard to land, tariff, and internal improvements—the American system of the nationalizing Whig party—was conditioned on frontier ideas and needs. But it was not merely in legislative action that the frontier worked against the sectionalism of the coast. The economic and social characteristics of the frontier worked against sectionalism. The men of the frontier had closer resemblances to the Middle region than to either of the other sections. Pennsylvania had been the seed-plot of frontier emigration, and, although she passed on her settlers along the Great Valley into the west of Virginia and the Carolinas, yet the industrial society of these Southern frontiersmen was always more like that of the Middle region than like that of the tidewater portion of the South, which later came to spread its industrial type throughout the South.

The Middle region, entered by New York harbor, was an open door to all Europe. The tide-water part of the South represented typical Englishmen, modified by a warm climate and servile labor, and living in baronial fashion on great plantations; New England stood for a special English movement—Puritanism. The Middle region was less English than the other sections. It had a wide mixture of nationalities, a varied society, the mixed town and county system of local government, a varied economic life, may religious sects. In short, it was a region mediating between New England and the South, and the East and the West. It represented that composite nationality which the contemporary United States exhibits, that juxtaposition of non-English groups, occupying a valley or a little settlement, and presenting reflections of the map of Europe in their variety. It was democratic and nonsectional, if not national; "easy, tolerant, and contented;" rooted strongly in material prosperity. It was typical of the modern United States. It was least sectional, not only because it lay between North and South, but also because with no barriers to shut out its frontiers from its settled region, and with a system of connecting waterways, the Middle region mediated between East and West as well as between North and South. Thus it became the typically American region. Even the New Englander, who was shut out from the frontier by the Middle region, tarrying in New York or Pennsylvania on his westward march, lost the acuteness of his sectionalism on the way.

The spread of cotton culture into the interior of the South finally broke down the contrast between the "tide-water" region and the rest of the State, and based Southern interests on slavery. Before this process revealed its results the western portion of the South, which was akin to Pennsylvania in stock, society, and industry, showed tendencies to fall away from the faith of the fathers into internal improvement legislation and nationalism. In the Virginia convention of 1829-30, called to revise the constitution, Mr. Leigh, of Chesterfield, one of the tide-water counties, declared:

One of the main causes of discontent which led to this convention, that which had the strongest influence in overcoming our venera-

tion for the work of our fathers, which taught us to contemn the sentiments of Henry and Mason and Pendleton, which weaned us from our reverence for the constituted authorities of the State, was an overweening passion for internal improvement. I say this with perfect knowledge, for it has been avowed to me by gentlemen from the West over and over again. And let me tell the gentleman from Albemarle (Mr. Gordon) that it has been another principal object of those who set this ball of revolution in motion, to overturn the doctrine of State rights, of which Virginia has been the very pillar, and to remove the barrier she has interposed to the interference of the Federal Government in that same work of internal improvement, by so reorganizing the legislature that Virginia, too, may be hitched to the Federal car.

It was this nationalizing tendency of the West that transformed the democracy of Jefferson into the national republicanism of Monroe and the democracy of Andrew Jackson. The West of the War of 1812, the West of Clay, and Benton and Harrison, and Andrew Jackson, shut off by the Middle States and the mountains from the coast sections, had a solidarity of its own with national tendencies. On the tide of the Father of Waters, North and South met and mingled into a nation. Interstate migration went steadily on—a process of cross-fertilization of ideas and institutions. The fierce struggle of the sections over slavery on the western frontier does not diminish the truth of this statement; it proves the truth of it. Slavery was a sectional trait that would not down, but in the West it could not remain sectional. It was the greatest of frontiersmen who declared: "I believe this Government can not endure permanently half slave and half free. It will become all of one thing or all of the other." Nothing works for nationalism like intercourse within the nation. Mobility of population is death to localism, and the western frontier worked irresistibly in unsettling population. The effect reached back from the frontier and affected profoundly the Atlantic coast and even the Old World.

But the most important effect of the frontier has been in the promotion of democracy here and in Europe. As has been indicated, the frontier is productive of individualism. Complex society is precipitated by the wilderness into a kind of primitive organization based on the family. The tendency is anti-social. It produces antipathy to control, and particularly to any direct control. The tax-gatherer is viewed as a representative of oppression. Prof. Osgood, in an able article, has pointed out that the frontier conditions prevalent in the colonies are important factors in the explanation of the American Revolution, where individual liberty was sometimes confused with absence of all effective government. The same conditions aid in explaining the difficulty of instituting a strong government in the period of the confederacy. The frontier individualism has from the beginning promoted democracy.

The frontier States that came into the Union in the first quarter of a century of its existence came in with democratic suffrage provisions, and had reactive effects of the highest importance upon the older States whose peoples were being attracted there. An extension of the franchise became essential. It was *western* New York that forced an extension of suffrage in the constitutional convention of that State in 1821; and it was *western* Virginia that compelled the tide-water region to put a more liberal suffrage provision in the constitution

framed in 1830, and to give to the frontier region a more nearly proportionate representation with the tide-water aristocracy. The rise of democracy as an effective force in the nation came in with western preponderance under Jackson and William Henry Harrison, and it meant the triumph of the frontier—with all of its good and with all of its evil elements. An interesting illustration of the tone of frontier democracy in 1830 comes from the same debates in the Virginia convention already referred to. A representative from western Virginia declared:

But, sir, it is not the increase of population in the West which this gentleman ought to fear. It is the energy which the mountain breeze and western habits impart to those emigrants. They are regenerated, politically I mean, sir. They soon become *working politicians;* and the difference, sir, between a *talking* and a *working* politician is immense. The Old Dominion has long been celebrated for producing great orators; the ablest metaphysicians in policy; men that can split hairs in all abstruse questions of political economy. But at home, or when they return from Congress, they have negroes to fan them asleep. But a Pennsylvania, a New York, an Ohio, or a western Virginia statesman, though far inferior in logic, metaphysics, and rhetoric to an old Virginia statesman, has this advantage, that when he returns home he takes off his coat and takes hold of the plow. This gives him bone and muscle, sir, and preserves his republican principles pure and uncontaminated.

So long as free land exists, the opportunity for a competency exists, and economic power secures political power. But the democracy born of free land, strong in selfishness and individualism, intolerant of administrative experience and education, and pressing individual liberty beyond its proper bounds, has its dangers as well as its benefits. Individualism in America has allowed a laxity in regard to governmental affairs which has rendered possible the spoils system and all the manifest evils that follow from the lack of a highly developed civic spirit. In this connection may be noted also the influence of frontier conditions in permitting lax business honor, inflated paper currency and wild-cat banking. The colonial and revolutionary frontier was the region whence emanated many of the worst forms of an evil currency. The West in the War of 1812 repeated the phenomenon on the frontier of that day, while the speculation and wild-cat banking of the period of the crisis of 1837 occurred on the new frontier belt of the next tier of States. Thus each one of the periods of lax financial integrity coincides with periods when a new set of frontier communities had arisen, and coincides in area with these successive frontiers, for the most part. The recent Populist agitation is a case in point. Many a State that now declines any connection with the tenets of the Populists, itself adhered to such ideas in an earlier stage of the development of the State. A primitive society can hardly be expected to show the intelligent appreciation of the complexity of business interests in a developed society. The continual recurrence of these areas of paper-money agitation is another evidence that the frontier can be isolated and studied as a factor in American history of the highest importance.

The East has always feared the result of an unregulated advance of the frontier, and has tried to check and guide it. The English authorities would have checked settlement at the headwaters of the Atlantic tributaries and allowed the "savages to enjoy their deserts in quiet lest the peltry trade should decrease." This called out Burke's splendid protest:

If you stopped your grants, what would be the consequence? The people would occupy without grants. They have already so occupied in many places. You can not station garrisons in every part of these deserts. If you drive the people from one place, they will carry on their annual tillage and remove with their flocks and herds to another. Many of the people in the back settlements are already little attached to particular situations. Already they have topped the Appalachian Mountains. From thence they behold before them an immense plain, one vast, rich, level meadow; a square of five hundred miles. Over this they would wander without a possibility of restraint; they would change their manners with their habits of life; would soon forget a government by which they were disowned; would become hordes of English Tartars; and, pouring down upon your unfortified frontiers a fierce and irrestible cavalry, become masters of your governors and your counselers, your collectors and comptrollers, and of all the slaves that adhered to them. Such would, and in no long time must, be the effect of attempting to forbid as a crime and to suppress as an evil the command and blessing of Providence, "Increase and multiply." Such would be the happy result of an endeavor to keep as a lair of wild beasts that earth which God, by an express charter, has given to the children of men.

But the English Government was not alone in its desire to limit the advance of the frontier and guide its destinies. Tide-water Virginia and South Carolina gerrymandered those colonies to insure the dominance of the coast in their legislatures. Washington desired to settle a State at a time in the Northwest; Jefferson would reserve from settlement the territory of his Louisiana Purchase north of the thirty-second parallel in order to offer it to the Indians in exchange for their settlements east of the Mississippi. "When we shall be full on this side," he writes, "we may lay off a range of States on the western bank from the head to the mouth, and so range after range, advancing compactly as we multiply." Madison went so far as to argue to the French minister that the United States had no interest in seeing population extend itself on the right bank of the Mississippi, but should rather fear it. When the Oregon question was under debate, in 1824, Smyth, of Virginia, would draw an unchangeable line for the limits of the United States at the outer limit of two tiers of States beyond the Mississippi, complaining that the seaboard States were being drained of the flower of their population by the bringing of too much land into market. Even Thomas Benton, the man of widest views of the destiny of the West, at this stage of his career declared that along the ridge of the Rocky mountains "the western limits of the Republic should be drawn, and the statue of the fabled god Terminus should be raised upon its highest peak, never to be thrown down." But the attempts to limit the boundaries, to restrict land sales and settlement, and to deprive the West of its share of political power were all in vain. Steadily the frontier of settlement advanced and carried with it individualism, democracy, and nationalism, and powerfully affected the East and the Old World.

The most effective efforts of the East to regulate the frontier came through its educational and religious activity, exerted by interstate migration and by organized societies. Speaking in 1835, Dr.

Lyman Beecher declared: "It is equally plain that the religious and political destiny of our nation is to be decided in the West," and he pointed out that the population of the West "is assembled from all the States of the Union and from all the nations of Europe, and is rushing in like the waters of the flood, demanding for its moral preservation the immediate and universal action of those institutions which discipline the mind and arm the conscience and the heart. And so various are the opinions and habits, and so recent and imperfect is the acquaintance, and so sparse are the settlements of the West, that no homogeneous public sentiment can be formed to legislate immediately into being the requisite institutions. And yet they are all needed immediately in their utmost perfection and power. A nation is being 'born in a day.' ... But what will become of the West if her prosperity rushes up to such a majesty of power, while those great institutions linger which are necessary to form the mind and the conscience and the heart of that vast world. It must not be permitted. ... Let no man at the East quiet himself and dream of liberty, whatever may become of the West.... Her destiny is our destiny."

With the appeal to the conscience of New England, he adds appeals to her fears lest other religious sects anticipate her own. The New England preacher and school-teacher left their mark on the West. The dread of Western emancipation from New England's political and economic control was paralleled by her fears lest the West cut loose from her religion. Commenting in 1850 on reports that settlement was rapidly extending northward in Wisconsin, the editor of the *Home Missionary* writes: "We scarcely know whether to rejoice or mourn over this extension of our settlements. While we sympathize in whatever tends to increase the physical resources and prosperity of our country, we can not forget that with all these dispersions into remote and still remorter corners of the land the supply of the means of grace is becoming relatively less and less." Acting in accordance with such ideas, home missions were established and Western colleges were erected. As seaboard cities like Philadelphia, New York, and Baltimore strove for the mastery of Western trade, so the various denominations strove for the possession of the West. Thus an intellectual stream from New England sources fertilized the West. Other sections sent their missionaries; but the real struggle was between sects. The contest for power and the expansive tendency furnished to the various sects by the existence of a moving frontier must have had important results on the character of religious organization in the United States. The multiplication of rival churches in the little frontier towns had deep and lasting social effects. The religious aspects of the frontier make a chapter in our history which needs study.

From the conditions of frontier life came intellectual traits of profound importance. The works of travelers along each frontier from colonial days onward describe certain common traits, and these traits have, while softening down, still persisted as survivals in the place of their origin, even when a higher social organization succeeded. The result is that to the frontier the American intellect owes its striking characteristics. That coarseness and strength combined with acuteness and inquisitiveness; that practical, inventive turn of mind, quick to find expedients; that masterful grasp of material things, lacking in the artistic but powerful to effect great ends; that restless, nervous energy; that dominant individualism, working for good and for evil, and withal that buoyancy and exuberance which comes with freedom— these are traits of the frontier, or traits called out elsewhere because of the existence of the frontier. Since the days when the fleet of Columbus sailed into the waters of the New World, America has been another name for opportunity, and the people of the United States have taken their tone from the incessant expansion which has not only been open but has even been forced upon them. He would be a rash prophet who should assert that the expansive character of American life has now entirely ceased. Movement has been its dominant fact, and, unless this training has no effect upon a people, the American energy will continually demand a wider field for its exercise. But never again will such gifts of free land offer themselves. For a moment, at the frontier, the bonds of custom are broken and unrestraint is triumphant. There is not *tabula rasa*. The stubborn American environment is there with its imperious summons to accept its conditions; the inherited ways of doing things are also there; and yet, in spite of environment, and in spite of custom, each frontier did indeed furnish a new field of opportunity, a gate of escape from the bondage of the past; and freshness, and confidence, and scorn of older society, impatience of its restraints and its ideas, and indifference to its lessons, have accompanied the frontier. What the Mediterranean Sea was to the Greeks, breaking the bond of custom, offering new experiences, calling out new institutions and activities, that, and more, the ever retreating frontier has been to the United States directly, and to the nations of Europe more remotely. And now, four centuries from the discovery of America, at the end of a hundred years of life under the Constitution, the frontier has gone, and with its going has closed the first period of American history.

FREDERICK JACKSON TURNER's original essay required popularization before its full impact was felt. Turner himself helped in that process, as did his students and eventually virtually the entire historical profession. In his later essays and lectures, concepts that appeared in germinal form in his first paper were expanded and reemphasised. The complete frontier thesis, as he understood it, can be understood only by extracting from these later works the passages revealing the evolution of the subject in his own mind. The pages that follow, written between 1896 and 1914, provide such a total picture. In them he stresses more fully than in his initial paper the effect of the frontier on American democracy, individualism, and a variety of traits of the national character.*

Later Explanations and Developments

It is important to understand, therefore, what were some of the ideals of this early Western democracy. How did the frontiersman differ from the man of the coast?

The most obvious fact regarding the man of the Western Waters is that he had placed himself under influences destructive to many of the gains of civilization. Remote from the opportunity for systematic education, substituting a log hut in the forest-clearing for the social comforts of the town, he suffered hardships and privations, and reverted in many ways to primitive conditions of life. Engaged in a struggle to subdue the forest, working as an individual, and with little specie or capital, his interests were with the debtor class. At each stage of its advance, the West has favored an expansion of the currency. The pioneer had boundless confidence in the future of his own community, and when seasons of financial contraction and depression occurred, he, who had staked his all on confidence in Western development, and had fought the savage for his home, was inclined to reproach the conservative sections and classes. To explain this antagonism requires more than denunciation of dishonesty, ignorance, and boorishness as fundamental Western traits. Legislation in the United States has had to deal with two distinct social conditions. In some portions of the country there was, and is, an aggregation of property, and vested rights are in the foreground: in others, capital is lacking, more primitive conditions prevail, with different economic and social ideals, and the contentment of the average individual is placed in the foreground. That in the conflict between these two ideals an even hand has always been held by the government would be difficult to show.

The separation of the Western man from the seabord, and his environment, made him in a large degree free from European precedents and forces. He looked at things independently and with small regard or appreciation for the best Old World experience. He had no ideal of a philosophical, eclectic nation, that should advance civilization by "intercourse with foreigners and familiarity with their point of view, and readiness to adopt whatever is best and most suitable in their ideas, manners, and customs." His was rather the ideal of conserving and developing what was original and valuable in this new country. The entrance of old society upon free lands meant to him opportunity for a new type of democracy and new popular ideals. The West was not conservative: buoyant self-confidence and self-assertion were distinguishing traits in its composition. It saw in its growth nothing less than a new

order of society and state. In this conception were elements of evil and elements of good.

But the fundamental fact in regard to this new society was its relation to land. Professor Boutmy has said of the United States, "Their one primary and predominant object is to cultivate and settle these prairies, forests, and vast waste lands. The striking and peculiar characteristic of American society is that it is not so much a democracy as a huge commercial company for the discovery, cultivation, and capitalization of its enormous territory. The United States are primarily a commercial society, and only secondarily a nation." Of course, this involves a serious misapprehension. By the very fact of the task here set forth, far-reaching ideals of the state and of society have been evolved in the West, accompanied by loyalty to the nation representative of these ideals. But M. Boutmy's description hits the substantial fact, that the fundamental traits of the man of the interior were due to the free lands of the West. These turned his attention to the great task of subduing them to the purposes of civilization, and to the task of advancing his economic and social status in the new democracy which he was helping to create. Art, literature, refinement, scientific administration, all had to give way to this Titanic labor. Energy, incessant activity, became the lot of this new American. Says a traveler of the time of Andrew Jackson, "America is like a vast workshop, over the door of which is printed in blazing characters, 'No admittance here, except on business.'" The West of our own day reminds Mr. Bryce "of the crowd which Vathek found in the hall of Eblis, each darting hither and thither with swift steps and unquiet mien, driven to and fro by a fire in the heart. Time seems too short for what they have to do, and the result always to come short of their desire."

But free lands and the consciousness of working out their social destiny did more than turn the Westerner to material interests and devote him to a restless existence. They promoted equality among the Western settlers, and reacted as a check on the aristocratic influences of the East. Where everybody could have a farm, almost for taking it, economic equality easily resulted, and this involved political equality. Not without a struggle would the Western man abandon this ideal, and it goes far to explain the unrest in the remote West to-day.

Western democracy included individual liberty, as well as equality. The frontiersman was impatient of restraints. He knew how to preserve order, even in the absence of legal authority. If there were cattle thieves, lynch law was sudden and effective: the regulators of the Carolinas were the predecessors of the claims associations of Iowa and the vigilance committees of California. But the individual was not ready to submit to complex regulations. Population was sparse, there was no multitude of jostling interests, as in older settlements, demanding an elaborate system of personal restraints. Society became atomic. There was a reproduction of the primitive idea of the personality of the law, a crime was more an offense against the victim than a violation of the law of the land. Substantial justice, secured in the most direct way, was the ideal of the backwoodsman. He had little patience with finely drawn distinctions or scruples of method. If the thing was one proper to be done, then the most immediate, rough and ready, effective way was the best way.

It followed from the lack of organized political life, from the atomic conditions of the backwoods society, that the individual was exalted and given free play. The West was another name for opportunity. Here were mines to be seized, fertile valleys to be preëmpted, all the natural resources open to the shrewdest and the boldest. The United States is unique in the extent to which the individual has been given an open field, unchecked by restraints of an old social order, or of scientific administration of government. The self-made man was the Western man's ideal, was the kind of man that all men might become. Out of his wilderness experience, out of the freedom of his opportunities, he fashioned a formula for social regeneration,—the freedom of the individual to seek his own. He did not consider that his conditions were exceptional and temporary.

Under such conditions, leadership easily develops,—a leadership based on the possession of the qualities most serviceable to the young society. In the history of Western settlement, we see each forted village following its local hero. Clay, Jackson, Harrison, Lincoln, were illustrations of this tendency in periods when the Western hero rose to the dignity of national hero.

The Western man believed in the manifest destiny of his country. On his border, and checking his advance, were the Indian, the Spaniard, and the Englishman. He was indignant at Eastern indifference and lack of sympathy with his view of his relations to these peoples; at the short-sightedness of Eastern policy. The closure of the Mississippi by Spain, and the proposal to exchange our claim of freedom of navigating the river, in return for commercial advantages to New England, nearly led to the withdrawal of the West from the Union. It was the Western demands that brought about the purchase of Louisiana, and turned the scale in favor of declaring the War of 1812. Militant qualities were favored by the annual expansion of the settled area in the face of hostile Indians and the stubborn wilderness. The West caught the vision of the nation's continental destiny. Henry Adams, in his History of the United States, makes the American of 1800 exclaim to the foreign visitor, "Look at my wealth! See these solid mountains of salt and iron, of lead, copper, silver, and gold. See these magnificent cities scattered broadcast to the Pacific! See my cornfields rustling and waving in the summer breeze from ocean to ocean, so far that the sun itself is not high enough to mark where the distant mountains bound my golden seas. Look at this continent of mine, fairest of created worlds, as she lies turning up to the sun's never failing caress her broad and exuberant breasts, overflowing with milk for her hundred million children." And the foreigner saw only dreary deserts, tenanted by sparse, ague-stricken pioneers and savages. The cities were log huts and gambling dens. But the frontiersman's dream was prophetic. In spite of his rude, gross nature, this early Western man was an idealist withal. He dreamed dreams and beheld visions. He had faith in man, hope for democracy, belief in America's destiny, unbounded confidence in his ability to make his dreams come true. Said Harriet Martineau in 1834, "I regard the American people as a great embryo poet, now moody, now wild, but bringing out results of absolute good sense: restless and wayward in action, but with deep peace at his heart; exulting that he has caught the true aspect of things past, and the

depth of futurity which lies before him, wherein to create something so magnificent as the world has scarcely begun to dream of. There is the strongest hope of a nation that is capable of being possessed with an idea."

It is important to bear this idealism of the West in mind. The very materialism that has been urged against the West was accompanied by ideals of equality, of the exaltation of the common man, of national expansion, that makes it a profound mistake to write of the West as though it were engrossed in mere material ends. It has been, and is, preëminently a region of ideals, mistaken or not.

Most important of all has been the fact that an area of free land has continually lain on the western border of the settled area of the United States. Whenever social conditions tended to crystallize in the East, whenever capital tended to press upon labor or political restraints to impede the freedom of the mass, there was this gate of escape to the free conditions of the frontier. These free lands promoted individualism, economic equality, freedom to rise, democracy. Men would not accept inferior wages and a permanent position of social subordination when this promised land of freedom and equality was theirs for the taking. Who would rest content under oppressive legislative conditions when with a slight effort he might reach a land wherein to become a co-worker in the building of free cities and free States on the lines of his own ideal? In a word, then, free lands meant free opportunities. Their existence has differentiated the American democracy from the democracies which have preceded it, because ever, as democracy in the East took the form of highly specialized and complicated industrial society, in the West it kept in touch with primitive conditions, and by action and reaction these two forces have shaped our history.

In the next place, these free lands and this treasury of industrial resources have existed over such vast spaces that they have demanded of democracy increasing spaciousness of design and power of execution. Western democracy is contrasted with the democracy of all other times in the largeness of the tasks to which it has set its hand, and in the vast achievements which it has wrought out in the control of nature and of politics. It would be difficult to over-emphasize the importance of this training upon democracy. Never before in the history of the world has a democracy existed on so vast an area and handled things in the gross with such success, with such largeness of design, and such grasp upon the means of execution. In short, democracy has learned in the West of the United States how to deal with the problem of magnitude. The old historic democracies were but little states with primitive economic conditions.

But the very task of dealing with vast resources, over vast areas, under the conditions of free competition furnished by the West, has produced the rise of those captains of industry whose success in consolidating economic power now raises the question as to whether democracy under such conditions can survive. For the old military type of Western leaders like George Rogers Clark, Andrew Jackson, and William Henry Harrison have been substituted such industrial leaders as James J. Hill, John D. Rockefeller, and Andrew Carnegie.

The question is imperative, then, What ideals persist from this democratic experience of the West; and have they acquired sufficient momentum to sustain themselves under conditions so radically unlike those in the days of their origin? In other words, the question put at the beginning of this discussion becomes pertinent. Under the forms of the American democracy is there in reality evolving such a concentration of economic and social power in the hands of a comparatively few men as may make political democracy an appearance rather than a reality? The free lands are gone. The material forces that gave vitality to Western democracy are passing away. It is to the realm of the spirt, to the domain of ideals and legislation, that we must look for Western influence upon democracy in our own days.

Western democracy has been from the time of its birth idealistic. The very fact of the wilderness appealed to men as a fair, blank page on which to write a new chapter in the story of man's struggle for a higher type of society. The Western wilds, from the Alleghanies to the Pacific, constituted the richest free gift that was ever spread out before civilized man. To the peasant and artisan of the Old World, bound by the chains of social class, as old as custom and as inevitable as fate, the West offered an exit into a free life and greater well-being among the bounties of nature, into the midst of resources that demanded manly exertion, and that gave in return the chance for indefinite ascent in the scale of social advance. "To each she offered gifts after his will." Never again can such an opportunity come to the sons of men. It was unique, and the thing is so near us, so much a part of our lives, that we do not even yet comprehend its full significance. The existence of this land of opportunity has made America the goal of idealists from the days of the Pilgrim Fathers. With all the materialism of the pioneer movements, this idealistic conception of the vacant lands as an opportunity for a new order of things is unmistakably present. . . .

This, at least, is clear: American democracy is fundamentally the outcome of the experiences of the American people in dealing with the West. Western democracy through the whole of its earlier period tended to the production of a society of which the most distinctive fact was the freedom of the individual to rise under conditions of social mobility, and whose ambition was the liberty and well-being of the masses. This conception has vitalized all American democracy, and has brought it into sharp contrasts with the democracies of history, and with those modern efforts of Europe to create an artificial democratic order by legislation. The problem of the United States is not to create democracy, but to conserve democratic institutions and ideals. In the later period of its development, Western democracy has been gaining experience in the problem of social control. It has steadily enlarged the sphere of its action and the instruments for its perpetuation. By its system of public schools, from the grades to the graduate work of the great universities, the West has created a larger single body of intelligent plain people than can be found elsewhere in the world. Its political tendencies, whether we consider Democracy, Populism, or Republicanism, are distinctly in the direction of greater social control and the conservation of the old democratic ideals.

To these ideals the West adheres with even a passionate determination. If, in working out its mastery of the resources of the interior, it has produced a type of industrial leader so powerful as to be the wonder of the world, nevertheless, it is still to be determined whether these men constitute a menace to democratic institutions, or the most efficient factor for adjusting democratic control to the new conditions.

Whatever shall be the outcome of the rush of this huge industrial modern United States to its place among the nations of the earth, the formation of its Western democracy will always remain one of the wonderful chapters in this history of the human race. Into this vast shaggy continent of ours poured the first feeble tide of European settlement. European men, institutions, and ideas were lodged in the American wilderness, and this great American West took them to her bosom, taught them a new way of looking upon the destiny of the common man, trained them in adaptation to the conditions of the New World, to the creation of new institutions to meet new needs; and ever as society on her eastern border grew to resemble the Old World in its social forms and its industry, ever, as it began to lose faith in the ideals of democracy, she opened new provinces, and dowered new democracies in her most distant domains with her material treasures and with the ennobling influence that the fierce love of freedom, the strength that came from hewing out a home, making a school and a church, and creating a higher future for his family, furnished to the pioneer.

The first ideal of the pioneer was that of conquest. It was his task to fight with nature for the chance to exist. Not as in older countries did this contest take place in a mythical past, told in folk lore and epic. It has been continuous to our own day. Facing each generation of pioneers was the unmastered continent. Vast forests blocked the way; mountainous ramparts interposed; desolate, grass-clad prairies, barren oceans of rolling plains, arid deserts, and a fierce race of savages, all had to be met and defeated. The rifle and the ax are the symbols of the backwoods pioneer. They meant a training in aggressive courage, in domination, in directness of action, in destructiveness.

To the pioneer the forest was no friendly resource for posterity, no object of careful economy. He must wage a hand-to-hand war upon it, cutting and burning a little space to let in the light upon a dozen acres of hard-won soil, and year after year expanding the clearing into new woodlands against the stubborn resistance of primeval trunks and matted roots. He made war against the rank fertility of the soil. While new worlds of virgin land lay ever just beyond, it was idle to expect the pioneer to stay his hand and turn to scientific farming. Indeed, as Secretary Wilson has said, the pioneer would, in that case, have raised wheat that no one wanted to eat, corn to store on the farm, and cotton not worth the picking.

Thus, fired with the ideal of subduing the wilderness, the destroying pioneer fought his way across the continent, masterful and wasteful, preparing the way by seeking the immediate thing, rejoicing in rude strength and wilful achievement.

But even this backwoodsman was more than a mere destroyer. He had visions. He was finder as well as fighter—the trailmaker for civilization, the inventor of new ways. Although Rudyard Kipling's "Foreloper" deals with the English pioneer in lands beneath the Southern Cross, yet the poem portrays American traits as well:

The gull shall whistle in his wake, the blind wave break in fire,

He shall fulfill God's utmost will, unknowing his desire;
And he shall see old planets pass and alien stars arise,
And give the gale his reckless sail in shadow of new skies.
Strong lust of gear shall drive him out and hunger arm his hand
To wring food from desert nude, his foothold from the sand.
His neighbors' smoke shall vex his eyes, their voices break his rest;
He shall go forth till south is north, sullen and dispossessed;
He shall desire loneliness and his desire shall bring
Hard on his heels, a thousand wheels, a people and a king.

He shall come back on his own track, and by his scarce cool camp,
There shall he meet the roaring street, the derrick and the stamp;
For he must blaze a nation's way with hatchet and with brand,
Till on his last won wilderness an empire's bulwarks stand.

This quest after the unknown, this yearning "beyond the sky line, where the strange roads go down," is of the very essence of the backwoods pioneer, even though he was unconscious of its spiritual significance.

The pioneer was taught in the school of experience that the crops of one area would not do for a new frontier; that the scythe of the clearing must be replaced by the reaper of the prairies. He was forced to make old tools serve new uses; to shape former habits, institutions and ideas to changed conditions; and to find new means when the old proved inapplicable. He was building a new society as well as breaking new soil; he had the ideal of nonconformity and of change. He rebelled against the conventional.

Besides the ideals of conquest and of discovery, the pioneer had the ideal of personal development, free from social and governmental constraint. He came from a civilization based on individual competition, and he brought the conception with him to the wilderness where a wealth of resources, and innumerable opportunities gave it a new scope. The prizes were for the keenest and the strongest; for them were the best bottom lands, the finest timber tracts, the best salt-springs, the richest ore beds; and not only these natural gifts, but also the opportunities afforded in the midst of a forming society. Here were mill sites, town sites, transportation lines, banking centers, openings in the law, in politics— all the varied chances for advancement afforded in a rapidly developing society where everything was open to him who knew how to seize the opportunity.

The squatter enforced his claim to lands even against the government's title by the use of extra-legal combinations and force. He appealed to lynch law with little hesitation. He was impatient of any governmental restriction upon his individual right to deal with the wilderness. . . .

But quite as deeply fixed in the pioneer's mind as the ideal of individualism was the ideal of democracy. He had a passionate hatred for aristocracy, monopoly and special privilege; he believed in simplicity, economy and in the rule of the people. It is true that he honored the successful man, and that he strove in all ways to advance himself. But the West was so free and so vast, the barriers to individual achievement were so remote, that the pioneer was hardly conscious that any danger to equality could come from his competition for natural resources. He thought of democracy as in some way the result of our political institutions, and he failed to see that it

was primarily the result of the free lands and immense opportunities which surrounded him. Occasional statesmen voiced the idea that American democracy was based on the abundance of unoccupied land, even in the first debates on the public domain.

This early recognition of the influence of abundance of land in shaping the economic conditions of American democrary is peculiarly significant to-day in view of the practical exhaustion of the supply of cheap arable public lands open to the poor man, and the coincident development of labor unions to keep up wages.

Certain it is that the strength of democratic movements has chiefly lain in the regions of the pioneer. "Our governments tend too much to democracy," wrote Izard, of South Carolina, to Jefferson, in 1785. "A handicraftsman thinks an apprenticeship necessary to make him acquainted with his business. But our backcountrymen are of the opinion that a politician may be born just as well as a poet."

The Revolutionary ideas, of course, gave a great impetus to democracy, and in substantially every colony there was a double revolution, one for independence and the other for the overthrow of aristocratic control. But in the long run the effective force behind American democracy was the presence of the practically free land into which men might escape from oppression or inequalities which burdened them in the older settlements. This possibility compelled the coastwise States to liberalize the franchise; and it prevented the formation of a dominant class, whether based on property or on custom. Among the pioneers one man was as good as his neighbor. He had the same chance; conditions were simple and free. Economic equality fostered political equality. An optimistic and buoyant belief in the worth of the plain people, a devout faith in man prevailed in the West. Democracy became almost the religion of the pioneer. He held with passionate devotion the idea that he was building under freedom a new society, based on self government, and for the welfare of the average man.

And yet even as he proclaimed the gospel of democracy the pioneer showed a vague apprehension lest the time be short—lest equality should not endure—lest he might fall behind in the ascending movement of Western society. This led him on in feverish haste to acquire advantages as though he only half believed his dream. "Before him lies a boundless continent," wrote De Tocqueville, in the days when pioneer democracy was triumphant under Jackson, "and he urges forward as if time pressed and he was afraid of finding no room for his exertions."

Even while Jackson lived, labor leaders and speculative thinkers were demanding legislation to place a limit on the amount of land which one person might acquire and to provide free farms. De Tocqueville saw the signs of change. "Between the workman and the master," he said, "there are frequent relations but no real association. . . . I am of the opinion, upon the whole, that the manufacturing aristocracy which is growing up under our eyes is one of the harshest which ever existed in the world; . . . if ever a permanent inequality, of conditions and aristocracy again penetrate into the world, it may be predicted that this is the gate by which they will enter." But the sanative influences of the free spaces of the West were destined to ameliorate labor's condition, to afford new hopes and new faith to pioneer democracy, and to postpone the problem.

The appeal of the undiscovered is strong in America. For three centuries the fundamental process in its history was the westward movement, the discovery and occupation of the vast free spaces of the continent. We are the first generation of Americans who can look back upon that era as a historic movement now coming to its end. Other generations have been so much a part of it that they could hardly comprehend its significance. To them it seemed inevitable. The free land and the natural resources seemed practically inexhaustible. Nor were they aware of the fact that their most fundamental traits, their institutions, even their ideals were shaped by this interaction between the wilderness and themselves.

American democracy was born of no theorist's dream; it was not carried in the *Sarah Constant* to Virginia, nor in the *Mayflower* to Plymouth. It came out of the American forest, and it gained new strength each time it touched a new frontier. Not the constitution, but free land and an abundance of natural resources open to a fit people, made the democratic type of society in America for three centuries while it occupied its empire.

To-day we are looking with a shock upon a changed world. The national problem is no longer how to cut and burn away the vast screen of the dense and daunting forest; it is how to save and wisely use the remaining timber. It is no longer how to get the great spaces of fertile prairie land in humid zones out of the hands of the government into the hands of the pioneer; these lands have already passed into private possession.

No longer is it a question of how to avoid or cross the Great Plains and the arid desert. It is a question of how to conquer those rejected lands by new method of farming and by cultivating new crops from seed collected by the government and by scientists from the cold, dry steppes of Siberia, the burning sands of Egypt, and the remote interior of China. It is a problem of how to bring the precious rills of water on to the alkali and sage brush. Population is increasing faster than the food supply.

New farm lands no longer increase decade after decade in areas equal to those of European states. While the ratio of increase of improved land declines, the value of farm lands rise and the price of food leaps upward, reversing the old ratio between the two. The cry of scientific farming and the conservation of natural resources replaces the cry of rapid conquest of the wilderness. We have so far won our national home, wrested from it its first rich treasures, and drawn to it the unfortunate of other lands, that we are already obliged to compare ourselves with settled states of the Old World. In place of our attitude of contemptuous indifference to the legislation of such countries as Germany and England, even Western States like Wisconsin send commissions to study their systems of taxation, workingmen's insurance, old age pensions and a great variety of other remedies for social ills.

The validity of the frontier thesis was questioned as early as 1925, but not until the end of the 1930s did it inspire its most effective critic. GEORGE W. PIERSON (1904–   ), Larned Professor of History at Yale University, has established himself as one of the most competent interpreters of the American past. His books range from discussions of Alexis de Tocqueville to the history of Yale University, where he earned both his undergraduate and graduate degrees. Pierson's quarrel is not only with the frontier hypothesis itself but with Frederick Jackson Turner. In several essays, of which this was the first published, he indicts Turner for faulty methodology, loose constructions, exaggeration, and paucity of exact definition; he also questions the hypothesis by suggesting that Turner failed to demonstrate the manner in which a brief pioneering experience could alter an entire civilization.*

► Turner's Views Challenged

It is now useful to ask two . . . questions of Professor Turner's essays: first, *how* (that is, by what means) did the frontier act on the frontier populations? And secondly, with what immediate *personal consequences?*

According to Turner the frontier influence tended, everywhere and at all times, to produce novelty in the form of new men, new institutions and new ideas—again with the further effect of modifying the men and institutions left behind on the sea-coast and in the countries of origin. Which is to repeat that the frontier took Europeans and made them into Americans, with consequences

of import even for those who remained European.

By what process or set of operations were those changes accomplished? Very curiously, Turner's essays are obscure on this point. Yet hints scattered here and there are perhaps explicit enough to warrant the statement that the all-important transformation between frontier exposure and American result was achieved in three different ways.

The first process was that of *starting over*, which was accomplished in a series of smaller steps: (a) by abandoning old—and essentially European—ways; (b) by returning to nature and to the simplest

* George W. Pierson, "The Frontier and Frontiersmen of Turner's Essays," *Pennsylvania Magazine of History and Biography*, vol. 64 (October 1940), pp. 454–478. The first one third of this article, which summarizes the frontier thesis, has been omitted. Printed without footnotes by permission of George W. Pierson and the *Pennsylvania Magazine of History and Biography*.

existence; and finally (c) by reconstructing society afresh, in the course of which reconstruction new ideas and new institutions were invented, new ways adopted, and an American society created. At first "the wilderness masters the colonist," Turner asserted. "American social development has been continually beginning over again on the frontier." Essentially, the West was a region whose condition resulted "from the application of older institutions and ideas to the transforming influences of free land. By this application, a new environment is suddenly entered, freedom of opportunity is opened, the cake of custom is broken, and new activities, new lines of growth, new institutions and new ideas, are brought into existence."

In cases where the inherited ideals and the traditional customs were too deeply ingrained in a settler-group to be obliterated, even by a howling wilderness, a different process took place. The old ways were *modified,* rather than abandoned, under the exposure to a new environment. In other words, this type of change was partial, and the Americanization consisted in deviation rather than in pure invention. Yet Turner was reluctant to allow that his irresistible force might have met some immovable object in the character of a particular population. In general, inherited peculiarities melted away before wilderness conditions. The Old West, Turner suggested, "diminished the importance of the town as a colonizing unit, even in New England."

The third means of Americanization, indicated in Turner's essays, was Americanization by *mixture.* Dissimilar men and institutions being brought into the same empty frontier zone, a sort of melting-pot process inevitably ensued. In any case, the result was a society differing from any (and from all) of its component factors. In the West, Turner pointed out, cross-fertilization was constantly going on. And if fusion was not perfect, nevertheless the most obdurate racial strains tended to lose themselves in the flood of migrating families. "In the crucible of the frontier the immigrants were Americanized, liberated, and fused into a mixed race, English in neither nationality nor characteristics."

One further proposition was advanced by Turner to explain the magnitude of the transformation accomplished in these three ways by the frontier. Observers had noticed, and Turner insisted, that for numberless individuals, as most certainly for American society as a whole, the frontier experience was a *repeated* experience. Over and over again the pioneer moved. A German family landing in colonial Pennsylvania might later move down the Shenandoah. The New Englanders in Michigan had come, not straight from Massachusetts, but in three jumps: first to Vermont, then to western New York, finally to Pontiac. Naturally, such repetition could not but strengthen the influence of the frontier, and each of the three processes—mixing, modifying, and starting over—were by renewed application intensified in power and in effect. The explanation seemed to Turner fully adequate to account for the results claimed.

By way of criticism it may be noted that the emphasis of the essays was apparently laid on the first process—the transformation by beginning over again. The reader almost gets the impression that the second and third explanations were offered only as a concession, only when reflection or discussion made it all too obvious that there never had been any real abandonment of many traits and institutions. Again, in passing, the question may be asked: were melting-pots and new environments to be found only at the hither edge of free land? Were they even confined to the West as a whole? Was there, by contrast, no population movement within the East? And no social blending? In a word, did the forest, or the Middle West, or all the unoccupied lands of the continent, have any monopoly—or even control the preponderant supply—of such disturbing and renovating forces? Yet, if not, what has happened to the unique rock-crushing and cement-mixing powers claimed for this Americanizing frontier?

The additional question then arises: whether our settlers, even on the real frontier, ever abandoned their ways and institutions completely, and—if so—whether the re-creation of society produced novelties in any substantial number? But this last problem is so fundamental and so very difficult that it may be a long time before the pertinent evidence can be gathered and fairly assessed.

Meanwhile, it is more illuminating and at least as pertinent to recall that Turner's essays were intensely concerned with the *personal* results of exposure to the wilderness. For the frontier experience was supposed to have produced the most thorough-going changes in human nature, as well as in society. Not merely did it break down old group arrangements and generate new institutions, particularly in the political and economic field; fundamentally and first of all it affected the emotions. A man was influenced in his attitude toward himself and toward his neighbor, toward God and toward nature, toward government domestic or foreign. And it was his new attitudes, very naturally and

very largely, that then determined his social development. Such at least was Turner's conviction; and he went into the matter with optimistic elaboration. Postponing, therefore, for another occasion the "Americanization" of our social institutions (the last part of the process), I proceed in this third section to a methodical restatement of how the frontier is supposed to have shaped American character.

Effects of the "Frontier" on Personal Attitudes

On one occasion Turner enumerated the intellectual products of frontier life as "that coarseness and strength combined with acuteness and inquisitiveness; that practical, inventive turn of mind, quick to find expedients; that masterful grasp of material things, lacking in the artistic but powerful to effect great ends; that restless, nervous energy; that dominant individualism, working for good and for evil, and withal that buoyancy and exuberance which comes with freedom. . . ." The statement has become classic, and illuminates Turner's own imaginative and exuberant mood. Yet his summary is not complete, and in orderliness of presentation it leaves a good deal to be desired. A more analytical catalogue seems, therefore, in order. This may be begun by reiterating that Turner's "frontier" affected men's attitudes, first of all toward themselves and toward all humankind.

The most obvious thing about the frontiersman's view of himself and of his place in the scheme of things was what Turner described as his *individualism*. The frontiersman of North America developed a supreme self-reliance. He was independent in thought and act; he believed himself capable for all emergencies; he had faith in himself and an unlimited confidence in the future. Let his neighbors also look out for themselves: the West was a free field of competition. "He honored the man whose eye was the quickest and whose grasp was the strongest in this contest: 'it was everyone for himself'." If, momentarily, some stranger proved to be the better man, the field was wide and his own chance would surely come. There was enough for all. In fact, the future could be nothing less than magnificent. "While his horizon was still bounded by the clearing that his ax had made, the pioneer dreamed of continental conquest. ... His vision saw beyond the dank swamp at the edge of the great lake to the lofty buildings of a mighty city." "The West caught the vision of the nation's continental destiny."

With such optimism, such faith in the economic future of the country, it was not to be wondered at that the settlers saw a chance "to rise to a higher plane of existence," and by their own unaided efforts. Every man could do it. "The self-made man was the Western man's ideal, was the kind of man that all men might become. Out of his wilderness experience, out of the freedom of his opportunities, he fashioned a formula for social regeneration, the freedom of the individual to seek his own."

Thus far, the individualism of the pioneer might be labelled optimistic and positive. Yet this individualism had its strong negative side as well. If the frontiersman was self-reliant, he was also impatient: impatient of restraint, suspicious of government, restless under authority. Anything that tied him down or controlled his actions aroused active resentment. He wanted to throw off the shackles of the eastern aristocrats, of

Europe, of his own past even—and be free. Civilization itself choked him. Not cultivation or the dead hand should rob the squatter of his new-won sovereignty. Intolerant of education and tradition, he distrusted all forms of order and restraint. Under his hands a complex institution was soon reduced to the family unit; society itself became atomic.

A second major characteristic of the frontier populations—there *democratic* attitude—seemed to Turner at least as noticeable as their optimistic or impatient individualism, and probably even more important. How could the settlers be independent, and socially cooperative, at one and the same time? Far from recognizing a contradiction here, Turner felt that the one was essentially a direct product of the other. For if a man respected himself, he also respected men in general. He believed not simply in himself but in the ideal of personal development for mankind as a whole; social discipline and aristocratic traditions alone were to be avoided: the frontier and the absence of government would allow each of his neighbors "to grow to the full measure of his own capacity." All of them hated monopoly, aristocracy, privilege. Each Westerner had faith in the plain man, tolerated equality of suffrage with his neighbor, and could cooperate gladly toward the realization of a common liberty and a mutual welfare. Thus it was that these pioneer individualists would come together in friendly neighborliness to vote, or to raise a dwelling, or to shuck the corn. And in this wise might it truly be said that "the frontier individualism has from the beginning promoted democracy."

On the democratic and tolerant neighborliness of Americans (as Westerners) Turner insisted over and over again.

Frontier areas were inimical to slavery, and were also the sites of equalitarian rebellion against other forms of monopoly. "Certain it is that the strength of democratic movements has lain chiefly in the regions of the pioneer." Conversely, of course, American democracy could not have had eastern or European origins. And in his essay on "The West and American Ideals," Turner nailed his convictions to the mast: "American democracy was born of no theorist's dream; it was not carried in the *Sarah Constant* to Virginia, nor in the *Mayflower* to Plymouth. It came out of the American forest, and it gained new strength each time it touched a new frontier...." On no other aspect of Americanism was Turner more insistent, or more certain of the explanation.

To recapitulate: The reconciliation between individualism and democracy was simple because the vast possibilities of the frontier made our democracy one of "mobile ascending individuals." Under the spell of the open spaces, the early Appalachian pioneer became an idealist. "He dreamed dreams and beheld visions. He had faith in man, hope for democracy, belief in America's destiny, unbounded confidence in his ability to make his dreams come true." With the later Mississippians, the story was still, and more confidently, the same: "The 'Men of the Western Waters' broke with the old order of things, . . . and proclaimed the ideal of democracy." . . .

˙ To attempt a critical analysis of the two concepts "individualism" and "democracy," within these brief limits, would betray a confidence in one's powers and an optimism as to the intentions of Providence almost "Western" in character—to say nothing of the disrespect for authority that such a course would

indicate. Certainly, to question the genuineness of "frontier individualism," or to cast doubt on the ancestry of democracy, must be recognized as rank lèse-Americanism.

Nevertheless, one or two observations may be offered. And if thereby any questions of fact or interpretation are raised, let the same be regarded not as attempts at conclusive judgments but rather as possibilities for the consideration of historical investigators.

In the first place, then, let it be observed that Turner nowhere exactly defines his two master words. Accordingly, each reader is forced to make his own translation. The problem at once arises: did Turner, by "democracy," mean to include under that heading *all* aspects of democracy? For example, did "democracy" mean a levelling, anti-privilege tendency that is sometimes called equallitarianism; or did the word mean freedom of first opportunity, whatever the ultimate inquality of rewards because of unequal talent or luck? If the emphasis was to be on equality and security, was it economic, or political, or social levelling that the frontier fostered? And what about the classes whose legal and political inferiority was so definitely maintained? Did pioneer women, for example, achieve the vote? Again, did even manhood suffrage suffice to prevent racial or class exploitation? In other words, did all frontier regions, or all frontier periods, pronounce the democratic credo in the same way, or come even close to laying the accent on the same syllables? Furthermore, if not, was there a common denominator which today can be detected and attributed to the influence of the wilderness experience? No doubt there must have been. But whether it should be understood in

Turner's vague and shifting terms seems much less certain. In any case, his thirteen essays offer assertion and warm appreciation: not definition and proof.

In similar fashion, the word "individualism" must sooner or later be put into some historical cyclotron, and broken down into its component elements. The operation will not be attempted here. Its necessity will merely be suggested by recalling an observation of Charles A. Beard, to the effect that on the particular frontier he had known there could be seen a lot of individuals, but little individualism. Another way of asking the same question would be to compare American individualism with French individualism of the more advanced type: that is, were our Westerners really scornful of public opinion? Or did they merely shrug off the social control of the East and the dead hand of the past, the while remaining vulnerable to the criticism of their fellow Westerners—still slaves as it were, but slaves to a tyranny of opinion that had become merely provincial? To persons who are acquainted abroad, it sometimes seems as if educated Frenchmen put more emphasis on independent judgment, and as if the rugged individualism which Turner celebrates had been considerably stronger on its economic than on its moral side. How account for the organizing and cooperative talents of the Americans consistently with any thoroughgoing moral or ideological individualism?

This brings us back again to our concept of "democracy," and to the statement of a final query. Was not the democracy of Turner's frontiersmen (as of Jefferson's followers) sometimes in part the expression of no government at all, rather than of a new kind of government? Was it not more closely related to anarchy than to a clearly formulated science of politics? On the other hand, when—or to the extent that—a theory can be detected (this time with applications to Jefferson's doctrine), did that theory really come out of the forest?

So much for the frontiersman's attitudes toward himself and his neighbors. Let us now examine his attitudes toward that forest from which he derived so many benefits. If Westerners were optimistic and idealistic about man, and acted accordingly, what opinion or line of conduct did they adopt toward nature?

The question should undoubtedly be stated in the plural, for man's reactions to the physical environment on the frontier were many and diverse. According to Turner, they ranged from a fierce destructiveness to a benevolent exploitation for the better comfort of man, from crude materialism to the purest idealism. The effect on nature, and in particular on the raw wilderness, was almost always the same: a brutal destruction and conquest and waste, so that at the end of three generations these masters of a continent of supposedly limitless resources found themselves driven to a policy of rueful conservation. For that half of the equation known as the frontier environment, the results of the presence of frontier populations have been so obvious as to make further comment superfluous. Turner, himself, regretted more than once the half unconscious, half wilful, but in any case all-too-successful efforts of the settlers to destroy the very thing that made them different and peculiarly American. Let us pass directly, therefore, to the qualities that the ill-fated American environment once engendered but now, presumably, can no longer produce.

On the frontier populations, the first effect of the raw wilderness was to call out all man's *courageous and aggressive propensities.* It was a sort of military training school "keeping alive the power of resistance to aggression and developing the stalwart and rugged qualities of the frontiersmen."

In the second place, the populations concerned experienced a new access of *energy, strength and ambition.* Turner even went so far as to insist that the encounter with new conditions and new problems beyond the mountains acted as "a tonic to this stock." Their very ideals, such as democracy, "came stark and strong and full of life from the American forest." Among the Southerners "a greater energy and initiative appeared."

In his treatment of the wilderness, accordingly, this new feeling of confidence and power made the frontier individualist increasingly *rough, ready and direct.* In his battle with the trees he needed no assistance from the state, no skillful mustering of the forces or the science of society. Here lay "such a wealth of opportunity that reflection and well-considered planning seemed wasted time." His own bare hands would make him master of all he surveyed. Squatter though he might be, his was an immediate and intoxicating sovereignty. Why even bother with the niceties of doing things, when primitive seizure worked so well?· "That method was best which was most direct and effective. The backwoodsman was intolerant of men who split hairs, or scrupled over the method of reaching the right."

This suggests the growth of another characteristic in the "frontier mind": a *disregard for niceties* or distinctions, a carelessness as to means, even a direct *contempt for ethical standards* of any restraining sort. If ancestral precepts or legislative statutes stood in the way, brush them aside. In the pioneer the law once again became personalized. On the negative side, when a crime was committed, it was "more an offense against the victim than a violation of the law of the land," and lynch law or vigilantes were the obvious remedy. On the positive side, a man was entitled to what he could take. Thus the frontier bred into Americans coarseness, brutality, and many related forms of immorality. Turner generally and conspicuously "refrained from dwelling on the lawless characteristics of the frontier, because they are sufficiently well known"; yet even he felt it necessary to mention the spoils system and other political laxities, the indifference to business honor and the increase in financial dishonesty, finally also the gambler and desperado— "types of that line of scum that the waves of advancing civilization bore before them."

The next group of characteristics derived from or emphasized by the frontier were of a different sort and might be classified all together under the head instability: an instability that was physical and intellectual as well as emotional.

Physically, the Westerner was astonishingly *nervous and restless.* Turner thought the colonials had been phlegmatic. If so, the contrast with the later pioneers was indeed sharp. For they were never still, never at peace, never content to take root and settle down. They were ever moving westward, chasing the game, following the frontier to some new purchase beyond the horizon. Sometimes it seemed as if it were change itself that they loved. Sometimes it took the path of political unrest, as if superabundant energies were turning into agitation.

Occasionally, there could be no question but that intellectual *adventurousness* had been aroused. For the Western settlers were full of curiosity, and visitors found them inquisitive to a degree. Under the stimulus of new problems at hand, and lured to discoveries just ahead, the Westerner sometimes became a Kiplingesque explorer, forever yearning after the unknown. In any case, a craving for novelty and a love of innovation got established in the blood of the American people.

Most obvious, however, was the emotional instability of the men of the woods and the open spaces. They were enthusiastic and angry, buoyant and despairing, humorous and deadly earnest by turns—but always *volatile and changeful of mood*. This characteristic was visible in occasional but excessive outbursts of religious feeling. They responded to the more "emotional sects" and were found a fertile field by the "Baptists, Methodists and later Campbellites, as by Presbyterians." Most of all they responded to emotional leadership in politics, and followed Clay or Jackson with a blindness of loyalty and an abnegation of personal thinking altogether extraordinary in so independent-minded and self-reliant a population. Turner called this the "leadership" principle of Western democracy. If it looks a little like a paradox, at least there can be no questioning the emotionalism involved.

The reader comes now to the *practical*

and materialistic qualities developed by the battle against the wilderness and by the long efforts to exploit the resources of nature. The struggle to survive in so raw an environment, according to Turner, emphasized the acuteness, the resourcefulness, and the inventive abilities in the human material. Again, the vastness of the country developed in its conquerors a taste for bigness, a belief in quantity, and a very unusual administrative capacity. Thence both materialism and managerial talent. The problems were so overwhelming, and the rewards so stupendous, that even individualism had to yield to the obvious advantage of organization. Accordingly, it should occasion no surprise, nor even too much regret, that in Ohio where yesterday the pioneer leaned on his ax, today the captain of industry sits enthroned. In any case, the materialism involved had been of a superior variety: "not the dull contented materialism of an old and fixed society," but the chance "to rise to a higher plane of existence."

Finally, Turner saw in the frontier the source of American dreams and of most of what was valid in *American idealism*. "In spite of his rude, gross nature, this early Western man was an idealist withal." "The very materialism that has been urged against the West was accompanied by ideals. . . . It has been, and is, preeminently a region of ideals. . . ." Turner devoted one whole essay to "The West and American Ideals," but his insistence went farther than that. Essay after essay returns to this proposition, paragraph after paragraph opens with the word "ideals," or with some confident echo of the heartening theme. To what ideals in particular did Turner refer? Primarily to beliefs or aspirations already mentioned: to the personal self-reliance, the economic optimism, and the political liberalism that so distinguished the West, especially in the Ohio and Upper Mississippi valleys. "The ideals of equality, freedom of opportunity, faith in the common man are deep rooted in all the Middle West." And what nourished the deep roots? "The ideals of the Middle West," answered Turner, "began in the log huts set in the midst of the forest a century ago." . . .

Once again a critical analysis is incumbent on American historians. In this case, unfortunately, even the most learned students of human nature as yet know so little about the motives of man, or the springs of his conduct, that no certainty or agreement can reasonably be expected. Moreover, it so happens that in this phase of his doctrine Turner once again managed to link his "frontier" with certain of the strongest traditions of the American people, as is sufficiently indicated by recalling that Americans have been almost fanatically proud of their freedom, their democracy, and their idealism. Furthermore Turner's explanation, in an age when the God of the Puritans no longer seemed to account for (or protect) American superiority, allowed historians and laity alike to continue to cling to the feeling that we were unique and chosen from among the nations. For a personal divinity, a natural force (the "frontier") had been substituted as source and justification. And to the support of his theory Turner had thereby drafted the equally strong current of American nationalism.

Whether or not this explanation seems adequate, the fact is obvious that more than intellectual interest today supports this portion of the Turnerian theory: the emotions have become involved. Just as in the case of his definition of "frontier," Turner's celebration of the "frontiersman" and his peculiarly "American" qualities has appealed to prejudices both national and local. It follows that the historian must be tentative, yet somehow retain his freedom to dissent. Perhaps it might be fair to begin the testing of Turner's conclusions in this matter by the application of internal logic and ordinary common sense—developing the argument in the first instance at the level of amateur observation and recorded opinion that Turner himself used. If such an examination were to be undertaken, the following questions might be usefully asked.

First, was Turner's list of American traits an acceptable list, or should it be modified by addition or omission? For example, were not money-mindedness and faith in education—to mention but two other traits—strongly enough developed in the United States to qualify in any list of Americanisms?

A second approach would be that of asking whether all of the acceptable list of Americanisms did indeed, so far as common knowledge or special investigation enables us to judge, derive orginally from a frontier experience or from the neighborhood or influence of a frontier area? For instance, was it the settlement of the Middle West, or even the bitter struggle against the stony soil of colonial New England, that engendered Yankee ingenuity? Patent Office statistics will hardly be found to support such a view. Again, were our managerial talents due entirely to the struggle against the wilderness? Or was not the opportunity for their exercise perhaps even greater in the area of manufactures and intensive farming? And what about origins? Bluntly, for Turner to treat economic individualism, or business abilities and materialism in general, without serious credit to the Commercial Revolution and the influence of European thought and capitalism, seems one-sided indeed.

In the third place, it ought to be asked whether the frontier did not perhaps produce qualities not emphasized in Turner's essays, and even positively reprobated by Americans in general? Among those omitted will doubtless be discovered certain less admirable traits; but that ought not to prohibit the question. In fact, it seems a fair guess that this method of approach to the frontier will repay a temperate investigator, particulary along the line of establishing a more balanced interpretation.

A fourth test might be quite clearly of the comparative type: if American individualism had its roots in empty land, how account for French individualism, or even for the sturdy love of liberty sometimes celebrated as a trait of English character? As much could be asked of other "American" traits. In other words, even should the frontier be accepted as a definite source, historians might yet do well to consider the other possibilities, before making so dogmatic and exclusive an attribution.

Finally, Turner's frontier essays should be "controlled" by comparisons of a somewhat different sort: for instance, by the study of other populations and other frontiers. Were the *habitants* of Lower Canada affected as were the Virginians or Vermonters by the American wilderness? Evidence is already being marshalled to indicate that the Pennsylvania Germans, at least, were not. Again, a comparison of rural opportunities with urban opportunities would appear decidedly useful. And additional suggestions could as easily be made. Perhaps enough has been said already, however, to establish a substantial doubt, and to indicate that this section of Turner's theory likewise needs a most thorough and painstaking overhauling.

In summary it should be observed that a large quarter of the thirteen essays still remains unanalyzed, and that in any case, prior to trial, doubts must not be stretched into established proof. Notwithstanding, it would already seem reasonable to recognize that Turner's "frontier" was a hazy and a shifting concept, riddled with internal contradictions, overlaid with sectional bias, and saturated with nationalistic emotion. Partly because of such preoccupations, and partly because Turner appears never adequately to have checked his literary deductions by a fresh and disinterested resort to the evidence, his conclusions as to the character and influence of the "frontier" must now seriously be brought into question.

Historians and economists had argued for several years over the validity of the safety-valve doctrine before 1945, when FRED A. SHANNON (1893–1963) added what was believed to be the *coup de grâce* in this tightly reasoned essay. The earlier discussion had apparently established two points: that a direct safety valve draining laborers westward in periods of depression had never operated and that the cost of moving to the frontier was high enough to exclude virtually all wageearners. To these early conclusions, Shannon added statistical evidence designed to show that after the Civil War, at least, the frontier did not even operate as an indirect safety valve by attracting Eastern farmers who might otherwise have become factory employees. Until his death Shannon was one of the nation's most respected economic historians. For many years he taught at Kansas State College and at the University of Illinois from 1939 until his retirement in 1961.*

Not Even an Indirect Safety Valve Attracting Eastern Farmers

Since 1935 there has been a growing suspicion among historians that the venerable theory of free land as a safety valve for industrial labor is dead. Out of respect for the departed one even the newer text books on American history have begun to maintain silence on the subject. For generations the hypothesis had such a remarkable vitality that a dwindling remnant of the old guard still profess that they observe some stirrings of life in the assumed cadaver. Consequently, it seems that the time has arrived for the reluctant pathologist to don his gas mask and, regardless of the memphitis, analyze the contents of the internal organs. Are the stirrings in the body an evidence of continued animation, or merely of gaseous and helminthic activity? Before the corpse is given a respectable burial this fact must be ascertained beyond any possible doubt.

There can be no question as to the venerable age of the decedent. Thomas Skidmore foretold him as early as 1829 in *The Rights of Man to Property!* George Henry Evans and his fellow agrarians of the 1840s labored often and long in eulogy of the virtues of the safety valve they were trying to bring into existence. The *Working Man's Advocate* of July 6, 1844, demanded the realization of "the right of the people to the soil" and said:

* Fred A. Shannon, "A Post-Mortem on the Labor-Safety-Valve Theory," *Agricultural History*, vol. 19 (January 1945), pp. 31–37. Reprinted without footnotes by permission of the Agricultural History Society.

That once effected, let an outlet be formed that will carry off our superabundant labor to the salubrious and fertile West. In those regions thousands, and tens of thousands, who are now languishing in hopeless poverty, will find a certain and a speedy independence. The labor market will be thus eased of the present distressing competition; and those who remain, as well as those who emigrate, will have the opportunity of realizing a comfortable living.

Long before Frederick Jackson Turner tacitly admitted the validity of the theory, even the name "safety valve" had become a middle-class aphorism. The idea was so old and so generally held that it was commonly repeated without question. The Republican Party had so long made political capital of the Homestead Act and its feeble accomplishments that the benefit to the industrial laborer had become an axiom of American thought. Turner, himself, made only incidental use of the theory as a further illustration of his general philosophy concerning the West. Apparently he made no effort to examine the basis of the safety-valve assumption. Had he done so, no doubt the theory would have been declared dead forty or fifty years ago, and the present autopsy would have been made unnecessary. It was some of the followers of Turner who made a fetish of the assumption, but in recent years few if any have gone so far as to say that Eastern laborers in large numbers actually succeeded as homesteaders.

The approach has been shifted. An early variation of the theme was that the West as a whole, if not free land alone, provided the safety valve. This, as will be seen, was no more valid than the original theory. Another idea, sometimes expressed but apparently not yet reduced to a reasoned hypothesis, is that land, in

its widest definition (that is, total natural resources), constituted a safety valve. This is merely one way of begging the question by proposing a new one. Besides, it is easy to demonstrate that as new natural resources were discovered the world population multiplied to take advantage of them and that the old problems were quickly transplanted to a new locality. It can readily be shown that the monopolization of these resources prevented their widest social utilization and that the pressure of labor difficulties was no less intense in new communities than in the old. Witness the Coeur d'Alene strike in Idaho in the same year as the Homestead strike in Pennsylvania. But the natural-resources-safety-valve theory will require a thorough statement and exposition by one of its adherents before an examination can be made. The manufacture of such a hypothesis will be a tough problem, in view of the fact that, ever since the development of the factory system in America, labor unrest has resulted in violently explosive strikes rather than a gentle pop-off of steam through any supposed safety valve. The question will have to be answered: If any safety valve existed why did it not work? Since it did not work, how can it by any twist of the imagination be called a valve at all?

Another turn of the argument is a revival of the supposition of Carter Goodrich and Sol Davison (further expounded) that while no great number of industrial laborers became homesteaders, yet the safety valve existed, because it drained off the surplus of the Eastern farm population that otherwise would have gone to the cities for factory jobs. So, free land was a safety valve because it drew *potential* industrial labor to the West.

Again, the question immediately arises:

Why did this potential safety valve not work? Was it really a safety valve at all or was it merely a "whistle on a peanut roaster"? There can be no confusion of definitions involved. There is only one definition of the term: "An automatic escape or relief valve for a steam boiler, hydraulic system, etc." Under the catch-all "etc." one may just as well include "labor unrest." Obviously the safety valve is not for the benefit of the steam, water, or labor that escapes from the boiler, hydraulic system, or factory. It is to prevent the accumulation of pressure that might cause an explosion.

A safety valve is of use only when pressure reaches the danger point. This is where the trouble comes with the labor safety valve in all of its interpretations. It certainly was not working at the time of the Panic of 1837, or in the depression following the Panic of 1873, when over a million unemployed workmen paced the streets and knew that free lands were beyond their reach. It was rusted solid and immovable during the bloody railroad strikes of 1877 and the great labor upheaval of the 1880s. When the old-time Mississippi River steamboat captain "hung a nigger" on the arm of the safety valve when running a race, it can be positively asserted that his safety valve as such did not exist. This belief would doubtless be shared by the possible lone survivor picked maimed and scalded off a sycamore limb after the explosion.

No responsible person has ever tried to deny that at all times in America some few of the more fortunate laborers could and did take up land. But this seepage of steam which went on almost constantly did not prevent the pressure from rising when too much fuel was put under the boiler, and the seepage almost stopped entirely whenever the pressure got dan-gerously high. It was not till the 1830s, when the factory system in America began to bloom and the labor gangs were recruited for the building of canals and railroads, that any situation arose which would call for a safety valve. The shoe-maker or carpenter of colonial days who turned to farming did not do so as a re-lease from an ironclad wage system, as millions between 1830 and 1900 would have liked to do if they could. It was an era of slipshod economy and easy re-adjustment, where no great obstacle was put in the way of misfits. Even if one admits that a scarcity of free labor for hire was one of the minor reasons for the late development of a factory system, and that the choice of close and cheap land kept down the supply, yet a far greater reason was the scarcity of manu-facturing capital. When the factory system began, it was easy to import ship-loads of immigrant laborers. The same could have been done a generation or two earlier if there had been the demand.

But perhaps a more substantial argu-ment is needed to answer so attractive a hypothesis as that of the potential safety valve. At first glance this new idea has some charm. Certainly the Western farms did not create their own population by spontaneous generation. If not Eastern industrial laborers, then undoubtedly Eastern farmers must have supplied the initial impulse, and each Eastern farmer who went west drained the Eastern po-tential labor market by one. But the question is: Did *all* the migration from East to West amount to enough to con-stitute a safety valve for Eastern labor? Did not the promise of free land, and such migration as actually occurred, simply lure millions of Europeans to American shores, seeking farms or in-dustrial jobs, the bulk of the newcomers remaining in the East to make possible a worse labor congestion than would have existed if everything west of the Mississippi River had been nonexistent? The answer is so simple that it can be evolved from census data alone. The post mortem can now be held. If a sufficient domestic migration did take place with the desired results, then there *was* a safety valve, and there is no corpse of a theory to examine. If not, then the theory is dead and the body can be laid to rest.

The first question to be answered is: How large a surplus of farm population developed and where did it settle between 1860 (just before the Homestead Act) and 1900 (by which date the last gasp of steam is admitted to have escaped from the safety valve)? Here close estimates must substitute for an actual count, for before 1920 the census did not distinguish between actual farm and nonfarm residence. But the census officials did gather and publish figures on the numbers of persons employed for gain in the different occupations, and, wherever comparisons can be made, it is noticeable that the ratio of farm workers to all other persons receiving incomes has always been relatively close to the ratio between total farm and nonfarm population. On this basis of calculation (the only one available and accurate enough for all ordinary needs), in forty years the farm population only expanded from 19,000,-000 to 28,000,000, while the nonfarm element grew from somewhat over 12,000,-000 to 48,000,000, or almost fourfold. Villages, towns, and cities gained about 18,000,000 above the average rate of growth for the Nation as a whole, while the farm increase lagged by the same amount below the average. These figures are derived from a careful analytical study of occupations, based on census

reports, which shows the number of income receivers engaged in agriculture creeping from 6,287,000 to 10,699,000, while those in nonfarm occupations soared from 4,244,000 to 18,374,000.

Small as was the growth of agricultural population, it must be noted further that over 35 percent of the farms in 1900 were tenant-operated, and 43 percent of all farm-income receivers were wage laborers. This leaves only 22 percent as owner operators. But even though 25 percent is conceded, this would allow only 7,000,000 people in 1900 living on farms owned by their families, except for some sons who were also wage laborers or tenants. But the total national population increase was nearly 45,000,000 in forty years. Though the zealot may choose to ignore the fact that at least *some* of the farm workers owned their own land even in 1860 and may accept the figure for 1900 as growth alone, yet he has put but a small fraction of the increased population of the United States on such farms anywhere in the Nation, and hardly enough to consider in the West. This is not the way safety valves are constructed.

A further analysis of the data reveals that only 3,653,000 farms in 1900 were operated, even in part, by their owners. But at the same time at least 21,000,000 farm people were tenants and wage laborers and their families on the total of 5,737,000 farms in the Nation. These laborers were rarely any better off financially (often worse) than the toiling multitudes in the cities. These were not persons who had found release either from the farms or the cities of the East on land of their own in the West. The bulk of them were still east of the Mississippi River. These were not *potential* competitors of the city workers. They were *actual* competitors, for the hard living conditions of each group had a depressing effect on the economic status of the other. Neither element had the opportunity, the finances, the experience, or the heart to try their luck in the West.

These incontestable facts and figures play havoc with the assumption that "perhaps most" of the Eastern boys who left their "ancestral acres" migrated "to the West to acquire and develop a tract of virgin soil." There just was not that much of an increase in the number of farms between 1860 and 1900. Only 3,737,000 units were added to the 2,000,-000 of the earlier year, and 2,000,000 of the total in 1900 were tenant-operated. How large a proportion of the Eastern boys who left their fathers' farms could have become by any possibility the owners of the fraction of the increase in farms that lay in the West?

Here the potential-safety-valve advocates spoil their own argument. One of them stresses the great fecundity of Eastern farmers, "a dozen children being hardly exceptional." At only the average rate of breeding for the whole Nation, the 19,000,000 farm population of 1860, with their descendants and immigrant additions, would have numbered about 46,000,000 by 1900. But barely 60 percent of that number were on farms anywhere in the country at the later date, and only 7,000,000 could have been on farms owned by themselves or their families. If farmers were as philoprogenitive as just quoted, then by 1900 the number of persons of farm ancestry must have been closer to 60,000,-000 than 46,000,000, and the increase alone would amount to at least 40,000,-000. But the growth of farm population was only 9,000,000, and, of these, little more than 2,000,000 could have been on farms owned by their families. If it could be assumed that all the augmentation in farm population had been by migrating native farmers, by 1900 there would have been 31,000,000 of farm background (as of 1860) residing in the villages, towns, and cities; 9,000,000 would have been on new farms or subdivisions of old ones; of these, nearly 7,000,000 would have been tenants or hired laborers and their families, depressing industrial labor by their threat of competition; and about 2,000,000 would have been on their own farms, whether "virgin soil" of the West or marginal tracts in the East. But it would be taking advantage of the opponent's slip of the pen to trace this phantasy further. The law of averages is enough in itself to annihilate the safety valvers' contention. By the use of this conservative tool alone it will be realized that at least twenty farmers moved to town for each industrial laborer who moved to the land, and ten sons of farmers went to the city for each one who became the owner of a new farm anywhere in the Nation.

As to the farms west of the Mississippi River, it is well known that many of them were settled by aliens (witness the West North Central States with their large numbers of Scandinavians). Here is a theme that might well be expanded. The latest exponent of the potential-labor-safety-valve theory declares that "potential labor was drained out of the country, and to secure it for his fast expanding industrial enterprise, the manufacturer must import labor from Europe." Anyone must admit that a fraction of the surplus farm labor of the East went on new farms. But how does this additional immigrant stream into the cities affect the safety valve? The immigrants may not really have increased the industrial population. It has often been contended that, instead, the resulting competition restricted the native birth rate in equal proportion to the numbers of the newcomers. Apparently this must remain in the realm of speculation. Be this as it may, the immigrants, with their background of cheap living, acted as a drag on wages, thus making the lot of the city laborer all the harder. This is not the way that even a *potential* safety valve should work.

But, returning to the West, there is a further fact to be considered. The total population west of the Mississippi River in 1860 was about 4,500,000. In 1900 it was just under 21,000,000. Surely the "fecund" Westerners must have multiplied their own stock to about 12,000,000 by the latter date. In the same forty years some 14,000,000 immigrants came to America. By 1900, with their descendants, they must have numbered half again as many, or 21,000,000, for it has not been contended that immigrant competition lowered the immigrant birth rate. On this point the census data are not altogether satisfying. Foreign-born persons and their American-born children (counting only half of the children of mixed American and alien parentage) numbered 23,673,000. No doubt the survivors of the foreign-born counted in the Census of 1860, together with their later children, would reduce the alien accretion since 1860 to the 21,000,000 estimate. If anyone can prove that that this should be cut still a few more million, he will not greatly change the estimates that follow.

The Western States, in proportion to their total population, had proved amazingly attractive to the immigrants. Though over 19,087,000 of the 1900 count (including those with only one foreign-born parent) lived east of the Mississippi River, 7,112,000 were in the States (including Louisiana and Minnesota) to the west of the same line. In the eleven Mountain and Pacific States they were 47.6 percent of the total population, the figure reaching 61.2 in Utah, 57.3 in Montana, and 54.9 in California. Nevada also had a majority. Kansas and Missouri alone of the West North Central group had less than 40 percent of alien parentage, while the percentage in North Dakota was 77.5, in Minnesota 74.9, and in South Dakota 61.1. In round numbers Minnesota had 1,312,000, Iowa 958,000, California 815,000, Missouri 741,000, Nebraska 530,000, Texas 472,-000, and Kansas 403,000. Aside from Texas the numbers, as well as the percentages, in the West South Central States were low.

In 1860 the trans-Mississippi West contained 653,000 persons of foreign birth, but the number of their American-born children was not given. Even if the survivors and the children numbered over a million, by 1900 those twenty-two States still had 6,000,000 of post-1860 immigrant stock. If the estimate for the increase of the pre-1860 element is too low, so, it can be countered, were the totals of the Census of 1900. Grandchildren were not counted, and mature immigrants of the 1860s could have had a lot of grandchildren by 1900. All the descendants of the pre-1860 immigrants were included in the estimate of 12,000,-000 for the increase of the inhabitants of 1860, whereas all after the first descent are excluded from the post-1860 immigrant posterity. On the other hand let it be conceded that 12,000,000 by internal expansion and 6,000,000 by immigration, or 18,000,000 in all, is too much. This would leave only 3,000,000 of the

West in 1900, or one-seventh of the total, accounted for by migration from the Eastern States. The calculator can afford to be generous. Subtract two million from the internal expansion and another million from the alien stock, and add these to the migrants from the Eastern States. Suppose, then, that 6,000,000 of the West's population of 1900 was of pre-1860 Eastern United States origin, and three times that many foreigners and their children had come into the East to replace them. It all simmers down to the fact that the West acted as a lure to prospective European immigrants, either to take up lands, to occupy vacated city jobs, or to supply the demands of a growing industry. In any case the effect was just exactly the opposite of a safety valve, actual or potential.

Now the question is in order as to how many of those Eastern boys who left their "ancestral acres" and migrated "to the West" actually were able "to acquire and develop a tract of virgin soil." As will soon be demonstrated, only 47.1 percent of the Western population of 1900 lived on farms. By the same ratio, a mere 2,826,000 of the exaggerated number of the Eastern stock (as listed above) were farm residents. There were barely more than 2,000,000 farms west of the Mississippi in 1900. If two-sevenths of the population was Eastern in origin, it may be assumed that the same proportion of the farming was done by them. This would give them less than 572,000 units to operate as owners, managers, tenants, or hired laborers. But in the West, as in the Nation as a whole, the ratio of tenants and hired laborers to all farmers was very high. A full 35 percent of all Western farms were occupied by tenants. The high ratio in the West South Central region affects the average

for all somewhat, but there were several other States that approximated the worst conditions. The percentage in Nebraska was 35.5, in Kansas 33.9, in Iowa 33.6, in Missouri 30.6, and in South Dakota 21.9. But, also, slightly over 40 percent of all Western farm-income receivers were wage laborers. If these same ratios apply to total population on the farms, then well over 1,130,000 of the Eastern element in the West were wage laborers' families; more than 989,000 were on tenant holdings; and less than 707,000 occupied farms owned by themselves. This means that there was only one person on such a family possession for each twenty-five who left the farms of the Nation in the preceding forty years. But perhaps this number is a little too small. No doubt a good number of the hired laborers were also the sons of the owners. Also, though many of the wage workers in the West lived with their families in separate huts on the farms, another considerable number were single men (or detached from their families) who boarded with the owner. How much this situation affected the given figures is uncertain. But here is something more substantial. Only 65 percent of the farms, or less than 372,000 in all, were owner-operated. Here, then, is the number of those tracts of "virgin soil" taken up and kept—one for each forty-eight persons who left their "ancestral acres" in the East, or possibly one family farm for each ten families. What a showing for the potential safety valve!

One point remains: Urban development in its relation to safety-valve theories. Between 1790 and 1860 the percentage of persons in cities of 8,000 or more inhabitants grew from 3.3 to 16.1; the number of such places from 6 to 141; and their population from 131,000 to 5,-000,000. Over half of this growth took place after 1840. The city was already draining the country. But this was only the curtain raiser for the act to follow. In the next forty years the number of cities was multiplied to 547, their inhabitants to 25,000,000, and their percentage of the total population to 32.9. They had grown more than twice as fast as the Nation at large. The same rule applies to all municipalities of 2,500 and over, as their population expanded from 6,500,000 to 30,400,000. The cities may have bred pestilence, poverty, crime, and corruption, but there is no evidence that they bred population that rapidly. Immigration alone cannot explain the phenomenon, for, if the entire number of immigrants after 1860 is subtracted from the nonfarm population of 1900, the remainder still represents twice the rate of growth of farm population.

It is conceded that the bulk of the immigrants settled in urban localities, and it has been demonstrated that the great bulk of the surplus of farm population did the same. For that matter, outside the Cotton Belt, the majority of the westward-moving population did not settle on farms. When the Eastern city laborer managed to pay his fare or "ride the rods" westward, he, like the migrating farmer, was likely to establish himself in a mining camp, town, or city, where, as in the Coeur d'Alene region of Idaho, he found that he had exchanged drudgery in an Eastern factory for equally ill-paid drudgery (considering living costs) in a Western factory or mine. The urbanized proportion of the population west of the Mississippi River, where 1,725,000 new farms had been created, very nearly kept pace with the national average. In 1900, when almost half (47.1 percent) of America's people were living in incorporated towns and cities, the ratio west of the Mississippi River was over three-eighths (38.1 percent). Minnesota exceeded, while Missouri, Iowa, and Nebraska nearly equaled the national ratio. The combined eleven Mountain and Pacific States rated even higher than Minnesota, with 50.6 percent of their population in incorporated places. It was only the Dakotas and the West South Central States that were so overwhelmingly rural as to keep the trans-Mississippi West below the national ratio. On the basis of the gainfully employed, always a better measure, the West showed a still higher proportion of nonfarm population. The census figures for 1870, 1890, and 1900 are used in the accompanying table to illustrate this point.

Persons Ten Years of Age and Over Gainfully Employed in the West, 1870, 1890, and 1900

Area	1870			1890			1900		
	Total	Agriculture		Total	Agriculture		Total	Agriculture	
	Thousands	Thousands	Percent	Thousands	Thousands	Percent	Thousands	Thousands	Percent
United States	12,506	5,922	47.4	22,736	8,466	37.2	29,286	10,438	35.7
Trans-Miss. West	2,199	1,170	53.2	5,811	2,703	46.5	7,717	3,642	47.1
W. N. Central	1,157	648	56.0	2,988	1,432	47.9	3,693	1,707	46.2
W. S. Central	628	417	66.4	1,487	933	62.7	2,322	1,472	63.4
Mountain	134	50	29.9	501	127	25.3	663	192	28.8
Pacific	280	65	23.2	836	212	25.4	1,039	271	26.1

In each decade, the War-Western regions were well below the national ratio of agricultural to town and city labor, and to 1890 they were far below. In 1870, outside the West South Central States and Iowa, the figure averaged 44.3 percent for seventeen Western States compared with 47.4 percent for the

United States. In the next twenty years, when free land was presumed to be the greatest lure of the West, the towns gained on the farms till the latter included only 46.5 percent of the Western total in spite of the still preponderantly rural character of the West South Central division. Then in 1890, according to the legend, the gate to free land flew shut with a bang, and the urban-labor safety valve rusted tight forever. Yet, the increase in agricultural population in the next ten years was nearly a fourth larger than the average for the preceding decades. Whereas the city had been draining labor from the farm before 1890, now that the theoretical safety valve was gone the Western farm was gaining on the Western city. Good land—free, cheap, or at speculators' prices—undoubtedly was more abundant before 1890 than afterward. Before that date, without cavil, this land had helped keep down *rural* discontent and unrest. A small percentage of surplus farmers, and a few other discontented ones in periods of hard times, had been able to go west and take up new farms, but many times that number had sought refuges, however tenuous, in the cities. Whether this cityward migration left the more intelligent and energetic or the duller and more indolent back on the farm is relatively immaterial so far as the release of pressure is concerned. Such evidence as has been uncovered shows no decided weight one way or the other.

This much is certain. The industrial labor troubles of the 1870s and 1880s, when this *potential* safety valve was supposed to be working, were among the most violent ever experienced in the Nation's history. Steam escaped by explosion and not through a safety valve of free land. On the other hand, down to 1890 the flow of excess farmers to the industrial centers was incessant and accelerated. When hard times settled down on the farms of the Middle West, as in the 1870s, Grangers could organize, anti-monopoly parties arise, and greenbackers flourish; but the pressure was eased largely by the flow of excess population to the towns. No doubt the migrants would have done better to stay at home and create an explosion. Instead, they went to town to add to the explosive force there. Farm agitation died down when a few reforms were secured, and the continued cityward movement retarded its revival.

However, after 1890 this release for rural discontent began to fail. The cities were approaching a static condition and were losing their attraction for farmers. This condition continued until between 1930 and 1940 there was virtually no net shift of population between town and country. In the 1890s when the city safety valve for rural discontent was beginning to fail, the baffled farmer was at bay. Drought in the farther West and congestion in the cities left him no direction to go. He must stay on his freehold or tenant farm and fight. Populism in the 1890s was not to be as easily diverted or sidetracked by feeble concessions as had been Grangerism in the 1870s. In the forty years after 1890, the farmers, balked increasingly in their cityward yearnings, began to take far greater risks than ever before in their efforts to conquer the arid regions. Four times as much land was homesteaded as in the preceding decades. Great things were accomplished in the way of irrigation and dry farming; but also great distress was encountered, great dust bowls were created, and great national problems of farm relief were fostered.

Generalization alone does not establish a thesis, but already there is a substantial body of facts to support an argument for the city safety valve for rural discontent. Nevertheless old stereotypes of thought die hard. Quite often they expire only with their devotees. It has been proved time after time that since 1880, at least, the old idea of the agricultural ladder has worked in reverse. Instead of tenancy being a ladder up which workers could climb to farm ownership, in reality the freeholder more often climbed down the ladder to tenancy. Yet there are people in abundance who still nourish the illusion that their old friend remains alive. There is no reason for assuming that in the present instance the truth will be any more welcome than it has proved to be in the past. There never was a free-land or even a Western safety valve for industrial labor. There never was one even of the potential sort. So far did such a valve fail to exist that the exact opposite is seen. The rapid growth of industry and commerce in the cities provided a release from surplus farm population. The safety valve that actually existed worked in entirely the opposite direction from the one so often extolled. Perhaps the growth of urban economy also, on occasion, was rapid and smooth enough to absorb most of the growing population without explosive effect. Once the people concentrated in the cities, there was no safety valve whatever that could prevent violent eruptions in depression periods. Of this, the die-hards also will remain unconvinced. The persons who mournfully sing that "The old gray mare, she ain't what she used to be" seldom are ready to admit that she never did amount to much.

The post mortem on the theory of a free-land safety valve for industrial labor is at an end. For a century it was fed on nothing more sustaining than unsupported rationalization. Its ethereal body was able to survive on this slender nourishment as long as the supply lasted. But when the food was diluted to a "potential" consistency, it was no longer strong enough to maintain life. Death came from inanition. The body may now be sealed in its coffin and laid to rest. Let those who will consult the spirit rappers to bring forth its ghost.

The reappraisal of the safety-valve doctrine by modern economists began in 1957 when Norman J. Simler reported to the Mississippi Valley Historical Association on "The Safety-Valve Doctrine Re-evaluated," a session long remembered because of the spirited discussion that followed between the author and two staunch anti-safety valvers, Fred A. Shannon and Murray Kane. It was carried a step further by two economists at the University of Washington, George G. S. Murphy and Arnold Zellner, whose articles on "Sequential Growth: The Labor-Safety-Valve Doctrine and the Development of American Unionism" in the *Journal of Economic History* for 1959 emphasized the necessity of viewing the whole economy, rather than any one segment, in determining whether the frontier had elevated wages. This entire controversy was reviewed by ELLEN VON NARDROFF whose appraisal of the arguments on both sides, and her own major contributions to the subject, seem to have settled the conflict—for the time being.*

A Resources and Sociopsychological Safety Valve

Eliminating the Monster

Perhaps the most remarkable thing about the so-called safety valve theory of the frontier is that scarcely a single detail of any of its many versions was seriously questioned until the mid 1930's. At that time, however, a sudden disillusion set in. Richard Hofstadter attributes it to the Great Depression which, he says, ". . . brought a revaluation of the frontier myth. Obviously the depression was world-wide, and the central problems confronting the United States were those of the world at large. The feeling that the Republic was not what it used to be led to the suspicion that it never had been."

It is also possible that not only the depression itself, but also the new breed of frontier philosophers it engendered gave soberer scholars some pause. A few of the wilder results of repopularization of the "Turner thesis" were enough to set almost any sane person affright. The resultant rash of debunking followed two main stratagems. The first held that the

---

* Ellen von Nardroff, "The American Frontier as a Safety Valve: The Life, Death, Reincarnation, and Justification of a Theory," *Agricultural History*, vol. 36 (July 1962), pp. 123–142. The latter portion of this article is printed without footnotes by permission of Mrs. Nardroff and the Agricultural History Society.

safety valve, or at least some of its essential functioning parts, never existed.

The first wound of this nature was inflicted on the "theory" in 1935 by Carter Goodrich and Sol Davison.[1] Using newspaper accounts of departures for or arrivals in the West as their principal source of information (supplemented by gleanings from state and local history, hotel registers, city directories, and records of immigration societies), they came to the conclusion that "too few industrial workers reached the frontier to attract notice in the accounts of settlement. What is even more striking, too few wage earners left the industrial centers to exert any marked effect on their labor situation." In this and in a later article, Goodrich and Davison make it clear, first, that they refer to the movement of industrial labor to the farm-making frontier. Secondly, they consider the results of their study a serious questioning of the notion that laborers took up farms in the West in absence of any evidence in favor of the notion, rather than as an outright refutal.

The ink was scarcely dry on the Goodrich/Davison articles when Murray Kane emerged with a similar argument which was more directly aimed. His attack on the safety valve "theory" was dual: (1) He insisted that it was impossible that eastern laborers could have become farmers because they didn't know how to farm. (2) Laborers could not migrate to western farms because they couldn't afford it; i.e., that they couldn't save enough out of wages.

While Davison, Goodrich, and Kane were questioning the existence of labor immigration to the West, the other half of the actual safety valve doctrine was also beginning to come under fire. It was

[1] The articles mentioned by Nardroff in this discussion are listed in the bibliography.

being suggested that there was no such thing as a free farm for labor to go to. While suggestions of this sort were being made casually during the middle and late 30's, the classic work by Clarence Danhof appeared in 1941. Dealing with the decade just prior to passage of the Homestead Act, he lists the following range of farm making costs prior to the first crop, the variations depending upon the area, what is included, and who reported the figures:

Size (in acres)	Minimum Cost	Maximum Cost
40	$440	$3,000
80	785	2,100
160	850	7,800

Danhof also strongly suggests that the land wasn't even very cheap in terms of the only two possible ways for laborers to accrue the necessary funds—savings from wages or credit. The former, he says, ranged from $1.00 to $2.00 per day and the latter was generally both short term and expensive.

All those who cast doubts on the efficacy of the farming frontier as a safety valve for industrial labor nonetheless assumed that what has previously been defined as a potential safety valve operated; i.e., that farmers in significant numbers chose to better their lot by taking up new farms for themselves and their sons in the West rather than sending their offspring off to the factories. Generally, their assumption was that, while the costs of migration may have deterred laborers, farmers could always exchange eastern improved farms for larger unimproved or semi-improved farms further to the West, thus indirectly holding up eastern wages. Fred Shannon changed all this. In 1936 he said:

Farmers might sell their eastern acres and

move West and so they did in order to provide farms for each of their sons, but the promise of cheap western land to the common laborer was as futile as a signboard pointing to the end of the rainbow.

By 1945, while not denying that farmers moved West, Shannon protested that the movement was not sufficient in quantity to counteract opposite tendencies and, therefore, to keep up industrial wages, at least not from 1860 to 1900. This was the case, he contends for two reasons: (1) "Ten sons of farmers went to the city for each one who became the owner of a new farm anywhere in the Nation." Put more broadly, while farm population increased by 50%, urban population quadrupled during the period. (2) Having generously estimated that 6,000,000 easterners of all kinds went West from 1860 to 1900, and observed that "Three times that many foreigners and their children had come into the East to replace them," he concludes: "It all simmers down to the fact that the West acted as a lure to prospective immigrants, either to take up lands, to occupy vacated city jobs, or to supply the demands of a growing industry. In any case the effect was just exactly the opposite of a safety valve, actual or potential."

Prior to Shannon's head-on assault on the actual and potential safety valves, the existence of one corollary to the former had been seriously questioned. As was indicated earlier, one notion of the effect of the active safety valve indulged by the professionals and actively espoused by New Dealers was that low wages in the East *drove* labor West. The assumption was, more explicitly, that migration westward accelerated during downturns of the business cycle. Goodrich and Davison, the first to consider a test of the assumption necessary, ap-

proached it by comparing the percentage of standard deviation in wholesale prices, cash sales of public lands and original homestead entries from 1830 (the earliest possible date industrial wage earners may be said to have existed) to the 1880s (just prior to the 1890 closing date of the frontier). Their conclusion was that probably depressions accelerated the extension of the farming frontier. While land sales and wholesale prices fluctuated together prior to 1860, the authors maintain that elimination of purely speculative buying might reverse the situation. Beyond 1860 the wholesale price and land acquisition curves fluctuate inversely, indicating increased farm-making during downturns in the business cycle.

Shortly thereafter, however, inspecting the 1837 panic, Murray Kane found that in the East the number and percentage of population engaged in manufacturing declined and the rate of increase in local agriculture rose, whereas the percentage increase in western population declined. He therefore concludes that the unemployed went, not west, but back home to grandpa's farm just outside of town to ride out the depression. In addition, he concludes that: "Conditions generally conspired to make immigration to the West overwhelmingly rapid during the prosperity period. As a rule the movement reached its peak just prior to the precipitation of the panic and contracted during the depression." This does not necessarily conflict with the data on which Goodrich and Davison's conclusions were based. During the period where their indices fluctuate inversely, they do so only at the beginning of the downturn in wholesale prices. This could be explained as a lag between Kane's eastern peak and its western manifestation. It also might be the result of delayed response of land prices in the East as compared to wholesale prices. (This is on the assumption that the farm-making shown was being done by farmers.)

The second general line of attack on the safety valve thesis maintains that if it did exist, it did not work as it was supposed to. The chief advocate of this point of view is Fred Shannon and his list of the things the defective or over-rated mechanism failed to do covers a wide range. One contention is that it made tenants and hired hands rather than farm owners out of those who entered western agriculture. Any number of people voiced a certain amount of restrained horror at the prevalance of western tenancy once it was exposed, but its alleged enfeebling effect on the safety valve is best stated by Shannon. After pointing out that in 1900 35 percent of all western farms were occupied by tenants and that over 40 percent of all western farm income receivers were wage laborers he adds:

Only 65 percent of the farms or less than 372,000 in all, were owner operated. Here, then is the number of those tracts of "virgin soil" taken up by and kept—one for each 48 persons who left their "ancestral acres" in the East or possibly one family farm for each 10 families. What a showing for the potential safety valve!

Secondly, there is the contention that the safety valve obviously didn't cure labor unrest. For one thing, there was *not* always full employment. The safety valve, in Shannon's words "certainly was not working at the time of the Panic of 1873, when over a million unemployed workmen paced the streets and knew that free lands were 'beyond their reach.'" (For all intents and purposes this is just another way of saying that the westward movement did not accelerate during de-

pressions). Moreover, American workmen discovered and used the strike, the safety valve notwithstanding. Again Shannon provides the classic statement with respect to the operating efficiency of the safety valve in this context. "It was rusted solid and immovable," he says, "during the bloody railroad strikes of 1877 and the great labor upheaval of the 1880s."

Still a third defect is noted; i.e., that the farming frontier safety valve didn't even cure rural unrest, which Richard Hofstadter calls "the dominant form of discontent in nineteenth century America." Rural unrest, according to Shannon, was temporarily relieved not by migration westward but cityward. He elaborates:

. . . Down to 1890 the flow of excess farmers to the industrial centers was incessant and accelerated. When hard times settled down on the farms of the Middle West, as in the 1870s, Grangers could organize, antimonopoly parties arise, and greenbackers flourish, but the pressure was eased largely by the flow of excess population to towns.

This urban frontier, he conveniently discovers, also closed around 1890, giving rise to what he insists were the much less easily assuaged demands of the Populist Movement.

Taming the Monster

When Fred Shannon culminated a decade of attack on the safety valve theory, he considered in his own words that he had conducted an autopsy and final burial of a creature that had been dead without knowing it for years. "Let those who will," he intoned in conclusion, "consult the spirit rappers to bring forth its ghost." This is unlikely to occur inasmuch as the alleged corpse is still very much alive and, as a result of the surgery conducted by Shannon and his predecessors, somewhat improved in appearance. To put the issue less metaphorically, most of the doubts raised during the '30s and '40s concerning the validity of the safety valve theory may be cheerfully conceded, not necessarily because they cannot be argued, but because they never were really worth arguing about. More precisely still, it should cause neither the general notion of a safety valve nor its less dogmatic adherents much pain to admit the following generalizations and conclusions:

1. The safety valve effect did not necessarily depend upon Eastern laborers going West to farms. Even Joseph Schafer conceded this much. ". . . It really cannot matter much," he says, "whether actual wage earners left their jobs to go West and take up lands if the westward movement kept the ranks of industrial labor thin enough to make it necessary for entrepreneurs to pay high wages instead of low wages." He might have added that it makes little difference if any specified group went West to do any one particular thing as long as somebody went West to do something which increased their productivity in relation to what it would have been in the East and if a high wage level were maintained as a result.

2. The frontier manifestly neither cured the business cycle nor remedied its effects. Such a concession merely denies that the safety valve responded to cyclical phenomena. It by no means denies a secular effect.

3. It is a patent fact that tenancy increased during a period when the frontier was extant and the safety valve presumably was operating. Again it does not matter what the Western immigrant did

upon arrival as long as he got there and did not worsen his condition in the process. There is not even any reason to believe that productivity would have been increased had the land concerned been held as a family farm by the tenant operating it. According to Paul W. Gates, one farming technique was agreed upon by landlords, tenants, and owners; i.e., mining the soil. There is also good reason to believe that tenancy drew more labor West than its absence would have. Gates, referring to estate accumulation in the West says: "It was these capitalist estate builders, whether cattle barons, land speculators turned developers, or men who went West with the set purpose of creating great plantations operated by tenants and hired hands, who made possible the employment of thousands of laborers." The only damage tenancy could have done to safety valvism was to dim a bit the idea of social fluidity, to dampen the socio-psychological version. This seems conceivable only if tenancy became predominant, as it did not, or if dramatic examples of individual success ceased. As Gates puts it, even those already in tenantry or the landless labor force "could still cherish the dream of owning a farm while they worked for others."

4. It is also relatively painless to amputate the segment of the safety valve thesis that says *free* lands are a *sine quo non* of its operation. Whatever the cost of western lands, two facts remain—they were cheaper than eastern lands, and the agricultural sector not only expanded during the frontier period (defined as up to 1900 or thereabouts) in terms of numbers of people engaged in it, but it expanded westward. In other words, free or merely cheap, somebody took them up. In any case, the cost of homesteading

was never claimed to be a serious deterrent to anything but eastern industrial labor.

5. It is undeniable that labor was not sublimely happy at all times and in all places. It is completely inconceivable that any economic development anywhere can take place without either periodic or localized maladjustment. On the other hand, that it did not usher in and maintain the economic millenium does not prove that the safety valve was not operating at all. The question essentially is not *whether* there was labor unrest. No one ever claimed that the frontier did more than mitigate discontent. The central proposition is that manifestations of labor unrest in the United States differed both in kind and degree from those elsewhere and that the frontier had something to do with it. This proposition has not been approached, much less attacked, by safety valve critics.

6. Oddly enough, a broad-minded safety valvist may also smugly concede the seemingly most devastating points in Fred Shannon's "Post-Mortem," namely that: (a) more farmers went to the city than went West, and (b) foreign immigration into the East more than replaced *all* those who migrated West. What Shannon forgets is that he is not talking about a static economy in either sector. While the agricultural sector was growing westward, the industrial sector was mushrooming both in the West and in the East. Those who came into the country by no means found themselves victims of underemployment. The jobs, actual or potential, vacated by those who went West were continually multiplying. The salient question is: did they multiply as fast as immigrants came in, and if so, was this development a direct or indirect result of westward expansion?

This question cannot be answered by Shannon's crude figures. The figures, therefore, are largely irrelevant. Norman Simler, the only person who seems to have done more than mumble "scissors" at Shannon since 1945, levels this same accusation in somewhat more explicit terminology:

To judge the importance of the West in this economic context one must not only look at what was happening on the supply side of the market. Here, one would have to admit that the labor supply function decreased over time independently of the reasons for which Eastern workers or potential Eastern workers, left the market; . . . In addition one must at least evaluate the absolute magnitude of the elasticity of demand for labor and the extent of the dynamic upward shifts in the labor-demand function. If both demand and supply displayed such dynamic shifts—I would guess that demand increased more than supply decreased—then the market position of workers became more favorable. To the extent that the West was a factor in this context, the safety valve was operating. . . . Given the relative shifts in the market functions over time, the wage elasticity of the functions is crucial. The more inelastic with respect to wages they are, the more favorable for the market position of the workers become the relative shifts in the functions.

In summary, we propose to concede that the actual or direct safety valve defined as movement of laborers to farms is and always was a ridiculous idea; and that the potential safety valve, defined as movement of farmers to farms, at best only partially illuminates the phenomena it was designed to explain. For all intents and purposes, what we are doing is tossing all aspects of what we defined as the simple safety valve, actual or potential, out the window. The question now is, where does it leave us? The answer is, right back where the safety valve theory first started, or at least, right back where Turner is said to have started with it. And like all others who have dabbled in the area, we have on our hands precisely the same proposition, consisting of precisely the same elements.

First, wages in the United States have always been high compared to elsewhere. This does not mean, as the more extreme anti-safety valvists seem to suggest rather desperately, that the worst paid worker in the U. S. A. does or ever did earn more than the best paid worker elsewhere. Neither does it mean that the depression wage level in the United States compares favorable with the prosperity level in other areas. What it does suggest is that, given a period longer than the business cycle, labor, on the average, received a proportionately higher share of factor payments at any given stage of economic development in the United States than elsewhere at a comparable stage. While there is little statistical evidence to support this contention, it is generally accepted that United States industry always has been extraordinarily capital intensive. Until this truism is disproven, it alone indicates either that labor was relatively dearer than capital or that American entrepreneurs were mad.

The term "high wages" also implies that real wages in the United States have always been higher than elsewhere at any given time. On the basis of the evidence that exists, it cannot be disputed that real wages in the colonial and early national periods were significantly higher in the United States than elsewhere at that time. Since real wages did not fall during the nineteenth century in the United States, it seems safe to assume that the level remained higher.

Even if someone can demonstrate that American workers were not really better off than their brothers elsewhere, the fact remains that, compared to other industrial working classes, they have tended to act as if they think they are. Call an American worker a proletarian and you may incite personal violence either because he doesn't know what it means and assumes it is derogatory, or because he knows what it means and is certain it's derogatory. In either case he is demonstrating the lack of developed class consciousness which has always been the despair of European socialist observers and which the socio-psychological safety valve, as described earlier, is supposed to have created.

The proposition still left to consider is that the frontier was a significant factor in producing the above phenomena. Before appraising the proposition itself, it is of utmost importance to avoid the pitfalls of earlier literature and specify exactly what this frontier is considered to be. It was two things. It was a process, a dispersion of population, capital, and a developing technology. It was the virgin area into which these elements moved and which they combined to develop. That area was not only vast, but capable of supporting a wide variety of kinds and intensities of economic activity.

Our proposition now reads: Did the process of developing this area contribute to the high wage level and the social outlook of the United States? And the answer becomes absurdly obvious. To respond other than in the affirmative is to reason that both would have been the same if United States development had been confined to the thirteen orginal colonies. The various safety valve "theories," however, were more nearly designed to answer the question of *how* the great continental frontier contributed.

Explaining how continental development mitigated class consciousness in North America consists largely in restating the socio-psychological safety valve theory and reiterating that it has never really been challenged in any systematic fashion. Two additional comments, however, should be made. Even if the multilingual, multi-ethnic nature of the American labor force is considered the prime deterrent to early unionization, this factor may be indirectly attributed to the frontier. It is generally maintained that mass immigration was the result of the pull of free land (actual or mythical) or of high wages. The former is obviously a frontier phenomenon. So is the latter, to the extent to which high wages are traceable to the existence of the frontier.

Of utmost importance to the socio-psychological safety valve notion is the effect of the frontier on the distribution of conventional symbols of wealth and status. In the western world no such symbol has been so important as the ownership of private property, especially land. In the early colonial period it was the ease with which land could be acquired that did much to lessen the awe with which the lower classes viewed their traditional betters. It is also suggested that even in later periods in the East, ownership of some bit of real estate was not only possible for large segments of the society (including wage earners) but quite prevalent in comparison to elsewhere. Land vacated in urban environs as commercial agriculture moved westward was at least available for homes. Even possession of a fifty-foot lot with a house of sorts and a couple of rows of radishes makes one a landowner.

We are now left with the effect of the frontier on the wage level, and propose to surmount this final hurdle by consolidating fragmentary expositions of the resources safety valve and asserting that it, also, has yet to be seriously challenged. The discussion can be most logically divided into the major components of wage determination: demand, supply, and productivity.

The effect of the frontier on the supply of labor to industry was due to the factor that has been most obvious all along; namely, that the agricultural sector was expanding physically. What some of the more violent anti-safety valvists would like to forget is that this is something of an anomaly in economic development. Both in Europe and in the typical underdeveloped country today, initial industrial development was and is based on exploitation of an agricultural labor surplus, meaning that the marginal productivity of labor in agriculture is or is approaching zero, that labor already engaged in agriculture may be withdrawn without reducing the total product of the sector significantly, and that the supply of labor to industry, for a time, at least, is infinitely elastic at subsistence wages. No such state of affairs ever existed in this country despite the fact that historians dearly love to use the term "surplus labor" without ever saying what they mean. As a result, American industry was relatively capital intensive from the start and continues to be so.

The absence of an agricultural labor surplus does not mean that agricultural labor could not be drawn into industry. Obviously it was. It seems safe to assume that the marginal productivity of labor in agriculture was rising so long as prime virgin land was available to exploit, fell as the soil was gradually mined and rose again with the application of improved technology. If at any time the productivity of labor in industry was rising faster or falling less fast than in agriculture, it could attract labor from the agricultural sector—but at a price higher than would have been obtained had not agricultural expansion rendered the supply of labor to industry less elastic. Like all such analysis, the above possibly assumes a greater mobility of labor than actually existed. However, immobility works both ways (as all kinds of safety-valvists have pointed out) and there is no reason to assume that one sector benefited more than the other.

It is true, on the other hand, that mass immigration was a partial substitute for the absence of an agricultural labor surplus and that as a result of immigration money wages fell in the nineteenth century. In other words, demand, in the form of high returns to labor in both agriculture and industry, seems to have created its own supply. However, the immobility principle may be invoked here with even more validity than in the domestic case. Whereas employment opportunities determined the *fact* of immigration, its *extent* was exogeneously determined. Given this, the competition for labor between two expanding sectors created a floor below which wages could not fall and two important characteristics of that floor should be delineated. First, the floor was low enough to permit industralization. As Kemmerer points out, had wages remained as high as in the colonial period, industrialization might well have been impossible. It seems unlikely that anyone would argue that the absence of an industrial sector would in the long run have benefited anyone—and least of all labor. Secondly, the floor was high enough to insure, as has been pointed out earlier, that real wages did not fall in the nineteenth century. It would seem, then, that endogeneous and exogeneous factors combined to balance demand with supply of precisely the right magnitude and elasticity to sustain expansion without lowering the standard of living of labor.

In a sense, the above analysis is an elaboration of the safety valve thesis. Unlike potential safety-valvists, however, we do not maintain that labor supply is the whole story.

In the preceding treatment of labor supply it is clearly indicated that the westward expansion of agriculture increased the productivity of labor in that sector. The same relationship exists between development of western resources in general and productivity in the industrial sector. As C. W. Wright pointed out long ago, obviously the productivity of all labor is higher when applied to abundant and prime resources. This effect, it should be added, does not necessarily depend on the number of people who migrate to the resources. So long as there is sufficient migration to maintain the extractive industries and the transportation system, the effect of the resulting abundance is the same on processing industries wherever they may be located.

One of Clarence Danhof's conclusions is that "fundamentally the productivity and profitability of eastern industry made high wages possible. Rapid growth guaranteed that such wages would actually be paid." Essentially, he is referring to the increasing effective demand of industry for labor. The growth on which this expanding demand was based was, of course, dependent on the rate of investment and the productivity of capital. In any underdeveloped country initial capital shortage is somewhat offset by the fact that marginal returns to capital are high. There is no reason to question that when the resource base is expanding the returns to capital will either increase or fail to diminish as soon as when the base is limited. It may well have been this extra yield which permitted the extensive expansion via "plowing-back" that was so characteristic of American industrial growth.

Industrial growth may also depend on agricultural growth. In the first place, an inadequate agricultural sector may be a bottleneck to industrialization purely and simply because it cannot support an urban working class. This was the case in Russia and is still one of their most bothersome problems. In many presently developing countries limited agricultural productivity is also a matter of prime concern. This was conspicuously not the case in the United States. As Louis Hacker points out:

The free lands of the West were not important, however, because they made possible the creation of a unique "American spirit"— that indefinable something that was to set the U.S. apart from European experience for all time—but because their quick settlement and utilization for the extensive cultivation of foodstuffs furnished exactly those commodities with which the U.S., a debtor nation, could balance its international payments and borrow European capital in order to develop a native industrial enterprise.

In other words, agricultural expansion westward not only supported industrialization and urbanization directly, it also indirectly contributed to a high rate of investment in the initial stages of industrialization.

In the above discussion we are by no means trying to imply that the mere fact of expansion into a frontier area will insure a high wage level or that it was expansion alone that sustained wages in the United States. Other people have expanded over vast areas with no such results. Such expansions arose from different social structures and different levels of technological development; and they expanded at different rates into different terrains. While varying degrees of emphasis may be placed on the institutional structure and technology from which migration proceeded in this country, we are suggesting that the net effect on the rate of economic growth and on wages of American expansion into the American West was positive.

Conclusion

In conclusion, one question seems inevitable. Why has analysis of the relationship of the frontier to the condition and outlook of the American worker been proceeding in so many divergent directions and down so many blind alleys for so long? It is impossible not to suspect that part of the difficulty lies in the fact that the issue, apart from the popular tradition, has been almost exclusively the property of historians and American historians at that. Thus, consideration of the topic has been limited both by professional tradition and by professional insularity.

The professional tradition that has been most debilitating is the assumption that the invention of safety-valvism was largely Turner's doing. Using Turner as a point of departure, two divergent cults have arisen which have inevitably found themselves at odds with one another. The first might be classified as Turnerism. Its doctrine involves acceptance of Turner as gospel and its professional output consists largely in adding footnotes to what Turner said or to what he might be construed to have said. The code of the second sect is most aptly termed Turneritis. Its practitioners, being somewhat allergic either to Turner or to those infected with what they diagnose as Turnerism, specialize in enumerating what Turner or his followers might have or should have done or said. Unfortunately, this branch of the literature is approximately 90 percent preachment and 10 percent practice. Few, if any, of its producers ever act on their own recommendations. Needless to say, neither Turnerism nor Turneritis has been very productive of new approaches to the problem.

Professional insularity has affected the work in this area in two ways. Firstly, the whole discussion has been provincially American to a large degree. While the over-all Turner thesis has been applied to physical expansions of other nations in particular and to the spread of Europeans in general, the conclusions of these applications have never really been sorted out and tied together. If they had been, such an effort would inevitably have indicated the direction that analysis of the effect of the American frontier on the labor force should have taken.

Secondly, the comparative work and techniques of other disciplines have been largely ignored. It is interesting to note in this connection that the few glimmers of real light thrown on the safety valve doctrine have emanated from the work of economists, or economic historians whose true loyalties are more attached to the adjective than to the noun in their professional label.

The other major obstacle which past writers on the subject of the safety valve have found almost impossible to surmount is the term itself. It is clearly too mechanistic to be descriptive of an organic process, but it is so much a part of professional jargon that its use, and the attendant problems arising therefrom, is almost impossible to avoid. Unfortunately, those who have recognized this obstacle (as Shannon undoubtedly did) have devoted too much energy to fighting the word and too little to unraveling the tangle it has helped create. Unfortunately, annihilating a word neither eliminates nor illuminates the phenomenon to which it refers.

We do not claim that our own brief analysis is totally free of traditional prejudice; nor do we pretend that it is final or even complete. We have not intended that it should be. What we have intended to do is first, to detect in previous literature and to restate the central issues which the safety valve doctrine was designed to illuminate; i.e., the relationship of the frontier to high wages and to the relative lack of class consciousness in the United States; secondly, to prune away the tangle of extraneous material which has concealed the basic anatomy of the safety valve doctrine from even its most dedicated fans; thirdly, to amputate the non-functional parts of that anatomy; and finally, to demonstrate a more fruitful method of examining what remains than has been employed in the past. Essentially what we suggest is that all attempts to explain the relationship of wages (or social attitudes) and the frontier solely in terms of human migration be abandoned. The phenomenon is an integral part of overall economic development in America and must be examined as such. Thus, the appropriate method of inquiry would consist of determining, first of all, how American economic development, with particular reference to the role of labor in that development, differed from that of other areas and other times; and then determining the role the frontier played in that difference; specifically to determine its influence on the rate of economic growth in relation to population growth and on the distribution of wealth and the symbols of wealth. It is obviously the opinion of the author that, as a result of such analysis, the net effect of expansion on the American wage level would be found to be positive. However, neither this opinion nor the details summoned to its support can be considered fully substantiated until more empirical evidence than now exists is summoned to their support. It is hoped that accumulation and application of such data is the task that will occupy future devotees of the safety-valve concept.

As for negatively disposed safety-valvists, charity demands that we focus directly on a proposition which so far has flickered only on the periphery of their attention; namely, that the most economical method of eliminating what remains of the safety-valve doctrine would be to undermine its foundations once and for all. Since no sane person would invoke the frontier or anything else to explain a non-existent phenomenon, if it were ever firmly established that in no relevant sense nor at any significant time were wages higher or the degree of class consciousness lower in the United States than elsewhere, the safety valve concept is not a cadaver to be buried, but an hallucination which will evaporate of its own accord. In this endeavor we wish the foes of safety-valvism Godspeed, but anticipate no great degree of success.

The standard of rebellion against Frederick Jackson
Turner's contention that American democracy originated on the frontier was raised in 1930 by
BENJAMIN F. WRIGHT, JR. (1900–   ), then
professor of government at Harvard University. He
argued that both the theory and practice of democracy
were well developed in Europe before being transplanted to the colonies and that most democratic
reform since that time originated in the East rather
than the West. After serving as president of Smith
College for a decade, in 1960 Wright moved to the
University of Texas as director of the American studies
program. The essay that follows represents a
pioneering attempt to restore some balance to the
frontier theory, which was overexpanded by some of
Turner's disciples.*

Democratic Practices
of English Origin

Perhaps the greatest shortcoming of
this frontier interpretation of our national development is its tendency to
isolate the growth of American democracy from the general course of Western
civilization. The proper point of departure for the discussion of the rise of
democracy in the United States is not
the American West but the European
background. The extent to which the
early colonies in this country reflected
the stage of development in their respec-
tive mother countries is especially significant. Consider, first, England and the
English colonies. Feudalism had been
virtually extinct in England for many
generations before the founding of New
England. Representative government had
been in process of development for at
least three centuries. The middle class
had risen to a position of independence
and power in the economic life of the
country, and was beginning to exercise a
large share of influence in things social
and political. The Protestant Reforma-
tion, one of the greatest factors in the
growth of modern democracy, was so far
advanced that a large proportion of the
English and Scottish were already dissenters from dissenters. In the English

* Benjamin F. Wright, "American Democracy and the Frontier," *The Yale Review*, copyright
Yale University Press, vol. 20 (December 1930), pp. 349–365. Reprinted by permission of Benjamin
F. Wright and *The Yale Review*.

colonies there were, with some temporary and relatively unimportant exceptions, almost no traces of feudalism, and independent land-holdings became the rule throughout most of the colonies. Representative government was almost immediately established in every colony. Brownism, Puritanism, Quakerism, and Presbyterianism, with their relatively decentralized and democratic forms of organization, were the religions of a large proportion of the colonists. With the striking exception of slavery, an institution virtually dead in the mother country, a great deal more than the bare beginnings of what we call democracy was planted in all of the English colonies in America. Some of them were, of course, considerably more democratic than others, and none of them would seem very liberal when measured by the standards of to-day, but all were in marked contrast to the institutions of neighboring colonies settled by people from other countries of Europe.

When France undertook the planting of colonies in the New World, feudalism was still a prominent feature of French social and economic life, although the political power of the feudal lords had been subordinated to the rise of centralized monarchy. In both theory and fact, France was a despotism; there was almost no self-government, local or national. The essentials of this system were transferred to Canada and remained there during the entire period of French control. In fact, as Professor Munro has shown, the seignorial system in Canada was, if anything, more like the French feudalism of an earlier period than that of contemporary France, and this paternalistic, undemocratic scheme of economic and social relationships outlived its parent stem in France. The religious system which the colonists brought with them retarded rather than promoted the development of a broader distribution of power and privilege. Representative government was not introduced until after the English took over the country and began to re-shape its institutions.

By the time of American colonization, Holland had developed a more liberal system of government than France, and the institutions of the New Netherlands were somewhat more democratic than those of New France. But they were considerably behind those of their English neighbors so far as concerned democratic government, and in the patroon system there was more of feudalism than ever existed in any English colony. The explanation is to be found in the fact that much of feudalism survived in Holland until well into the seventeenth century, and the patroon system is merely a version of the social and economic relationships then existing in the mother country.

The leading characteristics of the government of Spain in this period were centralization and the absence of representative or other effective checks upon the power of the crown. In neither economic nor social life was there much more of democracy, and the dominant church system was as rigidly controlled from a single centre as was the national political organization. The colonies settled by Spain in America fairly reflect this set of conditions. Government from above and a highly inflexible separation into classes continued throughout the period of Spanish control. The great haciendas, which are still an important feature of Mexican life, are remnants of the feudal order found in the land system of many of the Spanish colonies. As in the case of the English colonies, slavery was early introduced although it had virtually ceased to exist in Spain—the home government always objected to it, and it was due solely to the desires of the early generations of Spanish pioneers.

It is clear that the conditions which inevitably exist in frontier communities do set a temporary limit to the possibilities of such areas, but it would seem to be equally certain that they do not primarily determine the character of the institutions which are to be planted there. The customs and ideas brought by the settlers from an older civilization are of vastly more importance in shaping the history of the new lands. None of the American frontiers was ever "free from the influence of European ideas and institutions." The colonists who settled the first American frontiers altered remarkably little the principles which they inherited from their European ancestors. One group of colonists came with an autocratic, patriarchal, feudal or semi-feudal system and was well content to retain it. Another group settling just across an artificial boundary, where the character of the physical environment was not essentially different, brought with it the basic principles of democratic society and popular government. The frontier does not afford an adequate explanation of the system of independent land-holdings in the English colonies, the early development of representative government in Virginia, the New England town meeting, the tolerant democracy of Rhode Island, or Penn's liberal plans for the government and economic organization of his colony, any more than it accounts for the Canadian seignorial system, the great Mexican feudal estates, or the patroonships along the Hudson.

Now, it seems true enough that for more than two centuries the institutions of the frontier communities in what is to-day the United States were, with some exceptions, rather more democratic than those of the more densely settled areas. Life in the forest was usually a very primitive and a democratic life. But it does not follow, as Professor Turner has said, that the "forest philosophy is the philosophy of American democracy," or that "democracy came out of the American forest." The question is not whether the institutions of the American frontier were democratic but whether those institutions and the presence of the frontier were so influential upon the development of the institutions of the entire country as to justify such sweeping conclusions. And in determining the answer to this question, the first point to consider is how brief was the life of nearly all of these frontier communities as *frontier* communities, and how little in the way of permanent institutional influence it left behind after they ceased to be outposts of the westward advance.

According to the census definition, which Professor Turner presumably accepts, a frontier zone is one in which the population is less than two persons to the square mile. When the population becomes more dense, and when, one might add, settled agriculture or some form of industry succeeds hunting, fishing, trapping, nomadic grazing, and primitive agriculture as the principal means of gaining a livelihood, the area is no longer a frontier. With the change in the form of industry and in the density of population comes a resulting change in legal institutions and cultural life. The liberty, equality, and fraternity found among a scattered population engaged in wresting a scanty and precarious living from the forests, the streams, and the soil is not compatible with conditions in a more highly organized and stratified society. When the backwoods communities became populous centres or well-developed agricultural districts, much of the individual liberty of this life in the forests disappeared. At the same time, most of the social and economic equality and at least part of the fraternity found among the pioneers ceased to exist.

Throughout the Middle and Far West there are to-day scores of cities which fifty years ago were tiny outpost villages or parts of the unsettled tracts purchased from France or conquered from Mexico. Yet, for all their nearness to the frontier, they are ordinarily no more democratic in their ideals and institutions than similar cities in the East. In their economic life there is a similar concentration of wealth. Social stratification is as rigid as in the older centres. Government follows the same patterns both in its visible structure and in the invisible machine, which is usually the effective instrument of political control. In the agricultural population of these new States there is likewise little, if any, more democracy than in comparable regions of the seaboard States.

One of the most often repeated claims made for the frontier influence is that the presence of great areas of free land bounding the more populous sections promoted the development of democracy by affording a refuge for the oppressed and an opportunity for the ambitious. By thus draining off the surplus laborers of the settlements the exploitation of the working class and the consequent establishment of a stratified society was prevented. It is an assertion easier to make than to prove or disprove. During the greater part of the period in which democracy was developing most rapidly in America, there was a relatively heavy westward movement. How can we determine the extent to which the migration to the frontier was a cause of this development?

First of all, it should be pointed out that unoccupied land need not be free land, that is, land open to colonization. There have been frontiers of unsettled land scattered over many parts of the world which have been closed to settlement except under the strict supervision of the government controlling them. The unoccupied lands bounding the French and Spanish settlements in America were certainly not so free to the dissatisfied colonists as were those in the English colonies, nor were their ruling powers nearly so lenient toward westward migration as were the authorities of the regions occupied and governed by the English.

Nor is it clear that the westward migration has always been accompanied by the growth of democracy. During the century or more preceding the American Revolution the English communities grew from a few widely scattered settlements bordering the Atlantic to a group of well-populated colonies. The frontier line was pushed from the tide-water to the mountains, and even beyond. And yet, despite this almost continuous process of migration to the unsettled lands of the West, the development of democracy in the colonies moved at an extremely slow pace in this period. Indeed, recent investigations of its social history seem to indicate that, at the end of this westward expansion, the demarcation into social and economic classes was sharper than it had been three or four generations before. Indentured servitude existed throughout the colonies, and slavery flourished wherever it was economically profitable. The proportion of freemen exercising the right of suffrage or of holding office was little, if any, greater than it had been within a few years of the establishment of the settlements.

In other words, although the colonists brought with them a great deal more than the seeds of democratic society and popular government, their growth in this land of opportunity was far from being rapid. When the character of the people who came to America from England, and later from Scotland, Ireland, and Germany is taken into account—among whom there were few men of wealth, and nearly all were of the lower middle and lower class and with no established aristocracy—the process of institutional development becomes all the more difficult to understand if one relies heavily on the frontier interpretation. . . .

A favorite subject with those who hold the view that democracy came out of the West is the democratic character of the new state constitutions of this period. With some exceptions, the provisions of these constitutions were more democratic than those of the older States. In all probability the example of the new States was influential in accelerating the process of constitutional amendment in the older States. But with this said, the story is not complete. For in every instance of importance the principles that the Westerners applied were borrowed from the Eastern constitutions or from the political writings of Eastern Americans or Europeans. Thus the Westerners accepted the principle of a written constitution and the constitutional convention as the method of preparing the fundamental law, took over, usually without change, the bills of rights adopted during the Revolution, and altered but slightly the provisions for the frame of government which they copied from the earlier docu-

ments. They did, it is true, carry forward the movement for a broader suffrage, begun during the Revolution, but it is significant that they did not go beyond the ideal of many of the Revolutionary leaders, an ideal almost attained by a number of the original constitutions—manhood suffrage. And it is interesting to notice that Jackson's own State, Tennessee, was among the last to remove property qualifications.

Most spectacular and probably most important of the democratic movements of the time was that for the abolition of slavery. The crusading zeal of Garrison and other abolitionists did more than lead to war and the Thirteenth Amendment, for the emphasis throughout this agitation was upon natural rights, equality, and self-government. The result was to stereotype and sanctify in the minds of the American people the conception of democracy as an end in itself, of "government of the people, by the people, and for the people" as a condition which can and must exist in civilized society.

It is unquestionably true that the slavery issue involved the frontier, that the desire of North and South to gain control of the newly opened regions of the West intensified and embittered the entire controversy. But the struggle for the territories was result rather than cause. The underlying cause of the difference between North and South was in considerable part economic, but economic causes cannot explain the humanitarian idealism of the anti-slavery men. This enthusiasm for the cause of liberty and equality is, to quote Professor Schlesinger, "the American counterpart of a worldwide movement which had achieved the abolition of human bondage in Mexico and the other South American republics in the preceding decade, and which inspired Parliament in 1833 to provide for gradual eman.ipation in the British West Indies." The anti-slavery movement had many supporters in the new lands, but not all frontiersmen were in favor of emancipation. The slave-owners of the Southwest were just as truly frontiersmen as were the small farmers of the Northwest. Mississippi was as near to frontier conditions as Illinois, yet Jefferson Davis as fairly typified the general point of view in that State as Abraham Lincoln did in Illinois. Pioneering conditions prevailed over a large part of Texas, but it was one of the first States to secede and join the others banded for the defense of slavery, and it did so only after a popular referendum.

The general influence of the frontier in this country has probably gone toward entrenching and strengthening individualism, and particularly toward opposing governmental intervention to prevent the rapid exploitation of natural resources. However, it should be remembered that the dwellers in the new lands have not infrequently sought government aid for the building of roads, canals, and irrigation systems. And the strength of *laissez-faire* in America has been due as well to economic doctrines imported from Europe and to the relatively late coming of the industrial revolution. The recent tendencies toward social rather than individualistic democracy are much more the result of the machine age and of modern economic conditions than of the disappearance of the frontier. Since these conditions developed earlier in Western Europe than in America the trend toward social ownership, regulation, and guidance began

there earlier and has been carried further. Again, as so often in the past, the democratic movement in America is following in the paths of European experiments and European ideas.

And indeed the conclusion is unescapable that most of the significant aspects of our institutional development are to be interpreted adequately only in terms of the evolution of Western civilization. It seems safe to agree that, in this part of North America, the influence of the westward movement and of the example set by the pioneer communities did stimulate the growth of certain phases of democracy. But it appears even more certain that the most important elements in our democracy did not "come out of the American forest." It would be more nearly accurate to say that democracy came out of the East and found a congenial environment in the new areas. Its basic principles were carried in the *Susan Constant* to Virginia and in the *Mayflower* to Plymouth and in the thousands of vessels which followed in their wake. If they had brought different principles different institutions would have been developed.

Furthermore, of the ultra-democratic experiments tried out in the backwoods, those which endured and helped to influence the growth of American civilization were those most nearly in keeping with the course of development in the Western world as a whole. Certainly the frontier was never the only element in the process, and it was rarely more than a minor part of the total force which produced the degree of democracy attained in this country.

In the modern reappraisal of the frontier thesis, Turner has had no stauncher defender than JOHN D. BARNHART (1895–   ), of Indiana University. A lifelong student of the Midwest, Barnhart has edited the *Indiana Magazine of History* and has written, in addition to other books, a two-volume history of that state. His important work, *Valley of Democracy*, from which the extract that follows is taken, is based on a study of the governmental beginnings of states bordering the Ohio River. He concludes that the Western constitution-makers did borrow from Eastern documents but they tended to imitate practices that vested increasing power in the people. In this sense his writings serve as a corrective to Wright's thesis. They also emphasize the fact that Turner was speaking of *American* democracy, not democracy in general, when he generalized upon the frontier's influence.*

► # *American Democracy Distinguished from Democracy in General*

The Turner interpretation with its emphasis on American and frontier influences needs to be tested by the history of a definite place and time. For this purpose the story of the Ohio Valley . . . is well suited. It was an early part of our national history when the European heritage was still strong along the Atlantic coast, and the Ohio Valley included two Southern states where the plantation offered a competing way of life. The significance of the frontier is more clearly revealed when contrasted with the European influence in the East and the plantation system of the South.

Turner suggested that American history before 1890 was to a large degree the story of the colonization of the West. American development was explained by the existence of an area of free land, its continuous recession, and the advance of settlement westward. "Our early history is the study of European germs developing in an American environment," and "American social development has been continually beginning over again on the frontier." The source of its uniqueness was the fluid condition along the receding frontier where institutions were adapted to new circumstances.

In a few sentences Turner described the process. "The wilderness masters the

* John D. Barnhart, *Valley of Democracy: The Frontier versus the Plantation in the Ohio Valley, 1775–1818* (Bloomington, Ind., Indiana University Press, 1953), pp. 224–235. Reprinted by permission of John D. Barnhart and the Indiana University Press.

colonist. It finds him a European in dress, industries, tools, modes of travel, and thought. . . . It strips off the garments of civilization and arrays him in the hunting shirt and the moccasin. It puts him in the log cabin of the Cherokee and the Iroquois and runs an Indian palisade around him. Before long he has gone to planting Indian corn and plowing with a sharp stick; he shouts the war cry and takes the scalp in orthodox Indian fashion. In short, at the frontier the environment is at first too strong for the man. He must accept the conditions which it furnishes, or perish, and so he fits himself into the Indian clearings and follows the Indian trails. Little by little he transforms the wilderness, but the outcome is not the old Europe, not simply the development of Germanic germs. . . ."

Four divisions of frontier development have been described in the present study: first, the struggle of the frontiersmen east of the mountains to make the early Southern states more democratic; second, the early expansion of the frontier into and beyond the Appalachian Valley, and the efforts of the settlers to free themselves from Eastern control; third, the frontier of the southern half of the Ohio Valley, where two new states were formed after that area had freed itself from the Atlantic states; and fourth, the Northwestern frontier, where national policies rather than state policies were dominant.

In his article, "The Old West," Turner considered at some length the first of these frontiers in the years preceding the Revolution. He noted a westward movement of settlers from the Tidewater, the development of large estates, and the extension of the older aristocratic social order to the Piedmont and the Valley. From the north poured through the Val-

ley an extensive migration of Germans, Scotch-Irish, and other non-English settlers, who created a new continuous social and economic order which cut across artificial colonial boundaries and built a new South in contrast with the Tidewater. It was democratic, self-sufficient, primitive, and individualistic. It was characterized by the yeoman farmer, free labor, non-English settlers, and a multiplicity of Protestant sects. Recruits from the north strengthened the democratic forces and delayed the assimilation of the backwoods by the Tidewater society. Between the frontier and the coast a contest developed over the control of the state governments and their policies. Involved were the questions of currency, taxes, internal improvements, slavery, representation, franchise restrictions, and defense. The new state governments were more democratic because of this pressure, and the ideals of the Old West influenced the trans-Allegheny West. . . .

The second of the frontiers was described by Turner in "Western Statemaking in the Revolutionary Era." "Men who had lived under developed institutions were transplanted into the wilderness, with the opportunity and the necessity of adapting their institutions to their environment, or creating new ones capable of meeting the changed conditions." The pioneers preferred to establish government by social compact rather than to live under proprietary government or the control of large companies like the Vandalia Company. The presence of free lands broke down social distinctions, created economic equality, and promoted political equality, democracy, and individualism. There were four areas in the West where new governments were desired: the upper Tennessee Valley; the land between the Youghiogheny, Kanawha, and the Ohio; the combined Bluegrass basins of Kentucky and the Cumberland; and finally the Old Northwest. He briefly described the Watauga and Cumberland compacts, the proprietary experiment of Transylvania, the petitions of the Westsylvania settlers, the state of Franklin, and the early efforts of the Kentuckians to secure freedom from Virginia. Through these petitions and schemes of government ran certain ideas, such as "The people in an unoccupied land have the right to determine their own political institutions." Real grievances stimulated the efforts to secure independence from the East. Congress was expected, even urged, to assert control over the West and to permit the people to organize their own states within the nation.

Turner recognized the activities of speculators who were obtaining vast estates in the wilderness and establishing the foundations for a later aristocracy. Professor Abernethy has pursued this subject much further than Turner. He has suggested that many of the separatist movements were the work of the speculators rather than of the democratic frontiersmen, that the grievances were not very serious, that the frontier offered the speculators so much opportunity that the result was sometimes the encouragement of aristocracy rather than democracy.

Undoubtedly the initiative came from the speculators in a number of instances, but the hope of remedying frontier grievances rather than the initiative of the speculators gave life to the movements. In all probability historians have or will come to believe that the work of Abernethy necessitates a departure from the Turner point of view. Turner paid too little attention to the speculators and to the planter civilization of the South Atlantic states, which was endeavoring to dominate expansion into the lands beyond the Blue Ridge. The power of the older states was too great for the frontier associations and governments and the frontiersmen were defeated. The lack of victory does not disprove the democratic influence of the frontier, but merely makes it evident that it could not win under all circumstances. It must not be forgotten that frontier ideals were enunciated, that they were brought to the attention of Congress, and that they were embodied for a time in temporary governments.

In words that obviously referred to the early occupation of the southern half of the Ohio Valley, Turner wrote: "The 'men of the Western Waters' broke with the old order of things, . . . hotly challenged the right of the East to rule them, demanded their own States, and would not be refused, spoke with contempt of the old social order of ranks and classes in the lands between the Alleghanies and the Atlantic, and proclaimed the ideal of democracy for the vast country which they had entered." . . .

It is quite interesting that Turner began his career protesting the overemphasis upon European origins and insisting upon the importance of American influences but lived to be criticized for swinging the balance too far to the American side. His major suggestion was that the frontier, the process of beginning over again in that primitive environment, exerted the dominant forces in American history. Professor Benjamin F. Wright, of Harvard, declared that the greatest shortcoming of Turner's interpretation was its tendency to isolate the growth of American democracy from the general course of Western civilization.

No frontier was free from the influence of European ideas, Wright asserted, and the colonists altered remarkably little the principles inherited from Europe. Although he was unwilling to recognize the great influence of the frontier, he was inclined to hold its historian in part responsible for the strength of isolationism in the Middle West.

The suggestion that American democracy was essentially a product of the frontier was also rejected by Professor Wright. He insisted that the men of the Middle West were imitative, not creative, that their action seems to have accelerated the rate of growth of the democratic movement but not to have changed its direction, and that "the 'transforming influence' of the frontier, as it appears in Turner's essays, is largely a myth." He summarized his views by saying that "democracy did not come out of the American forest unless it was first carried there. On some frontiers democracy was not strengthened, rather the reverse."

Another Eastern criticism was written by Professor George W. Pierson, of Yale, who suggested that although the frontier influence may have been genuine, it has been exaggerated and magnified into a legend, and that Turner's views are no longer a safe guide to the student, but are sectional, emotional, and illogical. Pierson felt that some physical aspects of the frontier were inadequately considered but that free land was exaggerated and that the term "frontier" was not exactly defined. He questioned the transforming influence of the frontier, its individualism, and its promotion of democracy. . . .

The frontier was not a line or a place, but an area or zone where fluid economic and social conditions prevailed. A small density of population merely marked an area that was in its frontier period, when civilization was being reduced to the essentials by the wilderness and where the process of beginning anew was taking place. Turner may have used the term in different senses and even loosely, but this point ought not to be hard to grasp. Without it the Turner interpretation can have little meaning. Another deficiency in understanding the frontier influence is the lack of attention to the end of the pioneer period. Turner recognized the assimilation of the Piedmont by the civilization of the Tidewater by the time the Ohio Valley was able to take its place. The nature of the frontier period will appear more clearly when this is attempted for various sectional frontiers.

Another misconception that is quite pertinent to this discussion concerns the effect of the frontier upon democracy. The statement, "Democracy did not come out of the American forest unless it was first carried there," betrays a failure to read Turner's words with precision. Turner recognized the existence of theoretical democracy, of different types of democracy in other countries, and of the influence of Revolutionary ideas which he did not attribute to the frontier. He even observed that "the peculiar democracy of the frontier has passed away with the conditions that produced it. . . ." Is it not reasonable to point out that the frontier did not originate democracy, but rather those characteristics which made it Western or American? Of course, someone carried democracy to the frontier and to the forest in the beginning, but as it was carried to frontier after frontier, forest after forest, it was less European and more American. Democracy was carried on the *Susan Constant* and the *Mayflower,* but it was not American democracy. It was the European "germ" which Turner maintained was changed by its experience on the frontier until it ceased to be European and became American. Professor Wertenbaker's statement that American democracy was born in Westminster Hall should be taken in the same manner.

Perhaps this will appear a little clearer if the characteristics which distinguished the frontier or Western type from the European are noted. Turner frequently referred to equality, freedom of opportunity, and faith in the common man. These features, however, must be understood in the light of the frontiersmen's struggle against the aristocracy which controlled the colonial and state governments at the beginning of the Revolution. Frontiersmen thought that all would be well if they could destroy that control and establish a democracy of free men. Bonds of social caste, government favoritism, and hopeless inequality had to be destroyed—and the result would be equality. Freedom for the individual to work out his own destiny without artificial limitations or arbitrary obstacles constituted freedom of opportunity. Faith in the common man included the belief that the plain people were worthy of equality, of freedom, and of a share in government, that they possessed an intrinsic value and dependability which would enable them successfully to undertake the responsibilities imposed by these opportunities.

Finally, the occupation and development of government in the Ohio Valley was a story of conflict, of a struggle between aristocratic forces and democratic forces. Aristocracy was largely represented by planters, slave owners, and large speculators—men who were or who aspired to become large landholders, masters of slaves, and founders of established families. Their ideals did not include democracy or faith in the common people. Along the Eastern coast

they had insisted upon preserving as much as possible of the colonial aristocracy and had sought to retain the western lands under their control. In the West they endeavored, with the assistance of Virginia and North Carolina, to found an economic, social, and political order like that of the plantation South.

But the frontiersmen, who were generally poor, sought on each of the four frontiers to establish a democratic government which would be controlled by the common people in whom they had confidence. They failed in the South Atlantic states and in their earliest efforts beyond the Blue Ridge Mountains, but they were partially successful in the founding of Kentucky and Tennessee. North of the Ohio River, where they were not handicapped by state governments in the control of planters, they democratized the colonial system of the nation and founded three democratic states by 1820. The frontier had finally triumphed over the ideal of the English country gentleman as held in the South Atlantic states.

The story conforms very closely to the interpretation offered by Frederick Jackson Turner. Of the democratic influence of the frontier and its importance there is ample evidence. If the differences between American and European democracies are being sought, then the frontier influences should be studied, for in this case they are more significant. The history of democracy in the Ohio Valley reveals the differences between the civilizations of Europe and that of the United States and gives us an historical basis for the hope that we as people may continue to have a history of our own, a history that is unique.

Whether the frontier influences were more important than European will probably remain a matter of opinion and will not be susceptible of proof. Turner did not claim that democracy originated on the frontier, merely those characteristics which distinguished it from European democracy. The history of the Ohio Valley supports this point as well as the democratic influence of the frontier.

Finally, the story of the Ohio Valley where the democratic frontier forces struggled with the aristocratic ideal of the English country gentlemen is a unique story. The achievement of separation from the South Atlantic states, the democratization of the colonial system of the Northwest Ordinance, the establishment of majority rule in the new states, and the development of individualistic frontier democracy based upon faith in the common man are the notable accomplishments of the pioneers of the Ohio Valley.

When historians finally agree on the manner and extent to which the frontier altered American culture, they will base their conclusions largely on empirical evidence. A pioneering book in this area is *The Making of an American Community: A Case Study of Democracy in a Frontier County* (1959), by the University of Wisconsin historian MERLE CURTI (1897–   ). Selecting Trempealeau County, Wisconsin, between 1850 and 1880 because of the wealth of data available, Curti and a team of associates combed manuscript census and tax records for information that was fed into computing machines for analysis. The result is a volume that tends to substantiate the belief that the frontier exerted a positive influence on the evolution of democratic practices and attitudes. The book's conclusions are summarized in the selection that follows.*

The Impact of the Frontier: A Case Study

The non-English-speaking immigrant groups, however inferior in general economic status, did, as we have seen, get land—and on the whole as much land as the more favored native-born settlers. To this extent they had economic equality. Did political equality follow, as Turner predicted? We know that in each of the two decades after 1860 there was increasing participation of the foreign-born in politics. But the question whether this continued until there really was "political equality" our objective methods cannot answer. Perhaps we do not need objective methods to help us

get the answer to this question—it may be enough simply to look around us in our own communities.

Related to the subject of Americanization is our treatment of the property structure in the county. We found the same top-heavy distribution of total property in Trempealeau as in the group of Vermont townships when we analyzed all the property holders present in a given year. Of course the best comparison for our purposes would be with European communities, since most of our country was, in 1850, either frontier, recently frontier, or, a few short decades

* Merle Curti, *The Making of an American Community: A Case Study of Democracy in a Frontier County* (Stanford, Calif. Stanford University Press, 1959), pp. 442–448. Reprinted by permission of Merle Curti and the Stanford University Press.

back, frontier. But this comparison we could not make. We also found that particular nativity groups in the county, analyzed in the same way, showed a similar distribution, although some nativity groups were greatly inferior to others in average value of property reported. The top-heavy distributions that we found are, of course, evidence that complete democracy did not prevail on the Trempealeau frontier.

The matter appears in a different light, however, when we recall that the analysis of the total property of the *new* settlers of a given year revealed relatively small differences between the main nativity groups. Considering also that we found very few large speculators among new settlers and no evidence that there were at any time in this county the big estate builders that have been found elsewhere by others, we wonder if a study of the property structure of *all new settlers only* of a given census year might not reveal a less top-heavy distribution in Trempealeau than we found when we counted everyone. We should like to see this test made.

Our study of occupations has thrown revealing light on the degree of frontier democracy. For example, agricultural laborers and "farmers" not listed in the agricultural schedules of the census have been thought of as "have-nots," men without land in a place where land was supposed to be easy to get. But our study of the manuscript records showed that the great majority of the "farmers" without farms did have land, and that as a group even the farm laborers were by no means landless. Many of the latter were relatives of the householder, many were very young, many reported real property or farms or both. In other words, the percentage of farm labor in the farm

population of a given frontier census year is not necessarily a good index of landlessness on the frontier. We need further study of the "farmer" without improved land and the farm laborer in various frontier areas.

When we analyzed the changing economic fortunes of individuals and groups from decade to decade, we found evidence of phenomenal gains. Not only were there striking instances of individual economic gain in the period of early settlement, but between 1860 and 1870 practically all new settlers who remained in the county made striking advance. The farm people who remained in agriculture (and this was the great majority of them) made on the average a greater gain in value of total property than the town dwellers.

The rates of gain found for this same early decade, 1860 to 1870, confirmed our hypothesis of differential gain: the rate of gain for low-property groups was much higher than for high-property groups. The rich became somewhat richer, the poor became a good deal less poor. This finding offers no support for Marxist theory. It does constitute evidence of progress on this early frontier of groups initially very unequal, *in the direction of* economic equality.

Occupational changes too were in the predicted direction. Very few of the farm population who stayed in the county left agriculture. A good many in nonagricultural occupations maintained farms on the side and others left town for the farm.

We were particularly interested in the fortunes of those settlers who arrived before 1860 and stayed through 1870 and 1880. All of this group who remained active in farming gave evidence of success in agriculture. There may not have been an agricultural ladder, but there is no doubt that young farm workers of the 1860 census who stayed on in Trempealeau agriculture had a chance to climb upward, for almost all of them did so. All of the men who had been "farmers" without farms in 1860 had become farm operators by 1870. All but one of the young men who had started as farm laborers in 1860 were farm owners by 1880.

It is a matter of regret, of course, that we could not also study the later fortunes of settlers who left the county after one or two decades. Our study has shown that it was not only those who had little acreage or small amounts of property who left—there was great turnover in all age groups, all nativity groups, and all property groups. Two considerations seem to us important in dealing with the subject of turnover or persistence. First, it cannot be assumed that all or even most of those who left had failed or "given up," since moving was the order of the day. Second, many of those who settled in Trempealeau and made good there had lived in other places after leaving their initial homes. These were movers, like the ones who left Trempealeau for other places.

The economic slow-down of the 1870s raises the question whether the tremendous gains between 1860 and 1870 may not have been due to the postwar boom and not to frontier conditions. This question can be given final answer only by a comparison, using the same methods, between Trempealeau and nonfrontier areas in the same decade. We should like to see such a comparative study made. Meanwhile we can only say that it seems unlikely that gains as great *and as widespread* among the employed population as those we found could be due

solely to wartime prosperity. One reason why this seems unlikely is that the rate of gain of certain low-property occupational groups was about as high between 1870 and 1880 as for similar groups ten years before, in spite of the hard times in the latter decade.

We are thus brought back finally, in interpreting our data on economic standing and economic change in the farm population, to our theory that the kind and amount of change and advance we found in early Trempealeau would be likely to occur only under conditions offering very unusual stimulus and opportunity. We do not think, nor as a matter of fact did Turner think, that only a Western frontier could provide such conditions. We suggested in our chapter on the fortunes of new farmers that similar conditions might also be found in an area undergoing very rapid democratic industrialization or in one where a depression was followed by a period of full employment and the release of new energies and talents among the people. In our county, however, that stimulus and that opportunity were largely provided, we believe by frontier conditions.

It is difficult to say just how frontier experiences modified personalities that had been in greater or lesser degree shaped by the cultures of older parts of the United States and of the Old World. Young children who lived their formative years in the county during the frontier period might be expected to have developed personalities reflecting both the culture of parents and the actualities of the making of new communities. We cannot speak on this matter with benefit of quantitative findings, interviews, or projective tests, but we can still safely make certain points. The detailed and voluminous diaries of Alex Arnold, who came to Galesville as a youth, show that in his case the problems incidental to living in a new community sharpened certain traits and developed certain potentialities.

We can also report that the biographical and autobiographical material assembled by Judge Anderson, an immigrant who in his later years interviewed scores of still-living pioneers, gives some support to a thesis frequently presented in his newspaper by Samuel Luce. Editor Luce was not only an informed and sensitive spokesman for Trempealeau County, but he had wide and intimate knowledge of its people. With Judge Anderson, Luce believed that frontier experiences brought out or accentuated certain traits or potentialities in men, women, and children whose personalities obviously owed much to older cultures. These men again and again noted, and often gave specific examples to back up their observation, that frontier experiences in Trempealeau promoted self-confidence, optimism, resourcefulness, perseverance, a quickening of "mental faculties," and, especially, neighborly cooperation as well as individual initiative and sense of responsibility. We also may assume that this belief itself, frequently expressed in the newspapers, at old settlers' reunions, and on other ceremonial occasions, in some measure influenced behavior. For the belief must have tended to set up certain expectations of behavior in personal and social situations and tended to strengthen certain motives—notably those now referred to by some social scientists as affiliation and achievement motives.

While interrelationships between cultural heritage, frontier experience, and personality and values cannot be measured exactly, we can be assured of the great importance of the governmental blueprints that were at hand from the first. These blueprints provided rules and regulations for establishing representative county government, for making new towns as population increased, and for widespread male participation in decision-making at the town-meeting level. State government also provided judicial arrangements for handling personal and agricultural conflicts. All of these imported institutions provided a frame within which democracy was to be tested.

These institutions were subject to special strains inherent in the situations characteristic of the frontier experience in Trempealeau. One of the most important sources of strain was the dynamic nature of the population and of its distribution. The rapid development of the central and northern parts of the county raised the question of the relative roles in important decisions affecting the whole county of the newer northern majority and the older southern towns wishing to prolong their initial possession of the county seat. In somewhat the same way, the make-up of the Republican conventions was constantly being contested: at one time the smaller towns were overrepresented, at other times underrepresented. But out of sustained public discussion, voting and voting again, decisions were made, and remade, in accordance with the democratic principle of majority rule and consideration of minority interests.

A word here needs to be said about the demonstrated capacity of the Norwegian Americans, who formed the great majority in the new town of Pigeon, to come quickly and efficiently to terms with the democratic apparatus of the town meeting imported from New England to this frontier.

In one important respect the situation inherent in the Trempealeau frontier experience retarded for a time, at least in certain ways, the realization of the ideal of educational equality of opportunity: the children in the villages, the children of the families that were better off, and the children of American and British stock on the whole enjoyed greater opportunity than others to obtain such knowledge and skills as the public schools offered. With the development of better roads, the establishment of teachers' institutes, greater tax assets, and general acculturation, the disparity of the more pronounced frontier period lessened.

Believing that democracy means, among other things, multiple leadership, we asked what impact the frontier situations had on opportunity for leadership. It was clear that experience in leadership in older communities, amount of property on hand when migration to the county took place, and personal qualities all played an important part in leadership. But it is apparent that situations characteristic of the frontier also played a role. In that period before 1860 it was somewhat easier for young men to establish positions of leadership, in relation to the total population, than in the 1860s and especially in the 1870s. At all times, economic status counted; but the point to be made here is that, as our quantitative evidence shows, all sectors of the gainfully employed population were improving their status, both in the flourishing 1860s and even on the whole during the hard times of the 1870s, and all sectors furnished leaders. Further, while in the early period those born in non-English-speaking countries did not attain positions of leadership in proportion to the place their compatriots held in the total population, in the 1870s this situation was changing.

In sum, our study, both in its quantitative and qualitative aspects, lends support to what we believe are the main implications of Turner's thesis about the frontier and democracy, so far as Trempealeau County is concerned. It is indeed true that several important qualifications must be made—that for instance by some tests there was more democracy, as we defined it, in the 1870s than in the 1850s and early 1860s. But such qualifications are balanced by our findings which indicate that Turner's poetical vision of free land and of relatively equal opportunity was for a great many people being realized in Trempealeau County. The story of the making of this American community is a story of progress toward democracy.

The changing intellectual climate of the 1950s and 1960s fostered both a revival of belief in Turner's postulates and a newer and more healthy criticism of his thesis. Critics now quarreled less with his statements than with his assumptions. One who admirably represents this approach is EARL POMEROY (1915–   ), Beekman Professor of History at the University of Oregon, a lifelong student of the West, whose concentration on the post-pioneer period has led to such important books as *The Pacific Slope* (1965). In the article that follows, Pomeroy asks a pertinent question of the Turnerians: Was not the culture that pioneers carried westward a stronger force shaping their character than the wilderness environment? Had they not been guilty of underemphasising the influence of continuity in the molding of western civilization?*

The Significance of Continuity

The books we write about the West, a literary critic remarked recently, no longer explain our national history, no longer represent the historical possibilities of the West itself as they once seemed to do in the generation of Theodore Roosevelt and Frederick Jackson Turner. They may explain less because many historians of the West do not write well, and because many have narrowed the limits within which they write, even while investigators in other fields have broadened their inquiries and the West itself has greatly grown and changed. More fundamentally, most of those who write western history seem to assume that physical environment has dominated western life and has made the West rough and radical. Although he may scorn the popular appeal of the "Western" novel and motion picture, the historian has himself often operated within a formula, neglecting the spread and continuity of "Eastern" institutions and ideas.

It may seem sometimes that Turner gained recognition for western history as "a field for the serious study of the economist and the historian" only to open university doors to romanticists and antiquarians, who borrowed Turner's phrases rather than his methods and the range of

* Earl Pomeroy, "Toward a Reorientation of Western History: Continuity and Environment," *Mississippi Valley Historical Review*, vol. 41 (March 1955), pp. 579–591, 596–599. Printed without footnotes and with omissions by permission of Earl Pomeroy and the Organization of American Historians.

his imagination. In his time the environmental theory and the radical theme helped to integrate the story of the West into a more convincing pattern. Growing up in the Wisconsin fur-trading country, where Indian and European cultures still merged at the portage, he knew men who personified the impact of the forest. "The wilderness masters the colonist." He did his principal research on the West of the eras of Thomas Jefferson, Henry Clay, and Andrew Jackson, when the West seemed to spawn movements of protest that spread over the whole country. In his popular essays and in the classroom he pointed to the Populists as a contemporary example of western radicalism, once more disturbing and leavening the nation and demanding some new general synthesis or equilibrium that would incorporate some of the frontier into the whole.

The environmental interpretation appealed to Americans in a nationalistic and ostensibly democratic era, even though the nation was visibly becoming more like Europe in its drift to industrial power and an urban orientation of society. It had especial appeal when it elevated a century's romantic fascination with the western horizon, whether as promise or as threat, into the dignity of social science. Thus both Edward Channing and Turner, among other historians, set forth environmental interpretations of American history. Turner made the greater impact in part because of the unconscious assistance of others who were not historians but whose careers seemed to confirm his interpretation: Ignatius Donnelly, William J. Bryan, and Mary E. Lease, and later Robert M. La Follette, William D. Haywood, and Hiram W. Johnson.

Today the environmental-radical theme in western history has lost much of its appeal. To Turner the frontier was a cause that acted ultimately on the East; but now the effects that he thought he saw seem to have other causes, if they exist at all. American radicalism, such as it is, no longer looks to western centers like Madison, Lincoln, or Terre Haute; and in recent years as historians have turned increasingly to its history, perhaps with some of the nostalgia with which they looked at the disappearing frontier, the radicalism that they study is chiefly of the twentieth century—urban or at least post-frontier.

Though the old environmental-radical theme no longer seems so relevant to the present as it once did, it tends to govern the limits of western history-writing. While no longer finding (or, for that matter, seeking) the effects of environment that they once thought they found —the elements of western and national character that Turner described—historians still tend to concentrate on those aspects of the West where the impact of environment is clearest and sharpest. In so doing, they forget that they have performed an act of abstraction from a larger scene. They argue the importance of environmental influences in the West while demanding that the West qualify as West by being the place where environment predominates. They have run an irregular boundary line about the historical West that sometimes has to pass down the middle of city streets to avoid men and events that do not fit the formula. The line that they draw coincides with the antiquarian bias for localism, since under the primitive conditions of early settlement the outside world was less accessible than it shortly afterward became, and the immediate problems of subsistence had to find a largely local solution. Such limits prevail more generally among the popular histories and novels than among the works of broader framework noted in this paper, but they are familiar enough on university campuses as well as in the local journals. Courses and text books on the history of the West conventionally stop with the 1890s (though Turner extended his own course, History 17, well into the twentieth century); the mid-point of a representative college course in the history of California may be 1848, while miners and vigilantes dominate the "American period"; and in the published histories of western states the last chapters tend to become prim annals.

If we refuse to let another generation, in effect, force its interpretations on us by excluding such data as do not fit them, we may see that conservatism, inheritance, and continuity bulked at least as large in the history of the West as radicalism and environment. The Westerner has been fundamentally imitator rather than innovator, and not merely in the obvious though important sense that his culture was Western European rather than aboriginal. He was often the most ardent of conformists, although in times of imperfect communication he knew local standards better than national standards of conformity. Now it seems only natural that those major instruments of standardization, the motion picture and television studios, should have moved to the Pacific Coast, and that great state university systems as well as politicians who attack the freedom of inquery that universities live on should flourish most of all in western states.

The colonial everywhere, by virtue of his colonial status, tends to chafe against economic and political bonds, but he remains a colonial, which is to say a cultural transplant, often more traditionalist in attitude than his cousins in the older settlements. Such loyalty is not entirely a function of prosperity. If the emigrant prospered, he was no more interested in institutional change than was any other self-made man—often less interested, since it was so easy to believe that the country had grown up because of him, rather than he with it. In the West more than in the East, failure meant that a man had less contact with new ideas and with other men who might join him as reformers. The Westerner's perennial plea to the traveler to concede that the West had equaled or surpassed the East in schools, hotels, or civic virtue revealed the nature of his ambition. American culture often was diluted on the frontier, but often loyalty to it was strengthened. California, said *Overland Magazine* in 1883, "is in almost every respect an intensification of the American spirit. . . . All this is merely America, 'only more so.' "

Social change, however visible, was relative and irregular; different Wests often lived side by side, on the same street. While the on-rush of settlers seemed sometimes, as Henry R. Schoolcraft said, to tear up the old plan of life, still the raw frontier, which the settlers changed as they enveloped it, usually had been more in flux than the larger West behind it; and the disposition of the settlers was basically to conserve and transport what they had known before. Institutions and values changed less than geography, individual fortunes, and techniques. Even techniques often changed little as transportation improved. Institutional changes might have been greater if the men who led the West had sought a new country more than they sought individual self-realization and self improvement. In general they were neither refugees nor entirely exiles. New York or Pennsylvania was still a second home. Coming in hope rather than in fear or bitterness, often with some small stake for the new venture, members of a fairly homogeneous culture, they had little in common with Indians moved from their hereditary lands, or with convicts transported from Europe. Seeing the vigor of individual aspiration, historians sometimes have assumed too readily that Westerners wished to cut themselves off from eastern ways, much as historians once exaggerated the antipathy of colonial Puritans to England and the Anglican church. In fact most attempts to illustrate the western spirit by referring to large and purposeful institutional innovations are likely to break down.

In the field of government and politics, most clearly of all, it is evident that western history has been constricted by a local framework that has slighted similarities, antecedents, and outside influences generally. Territorial government, which clearly was the instrument of Congress, has been described with more attention to establishment than to operation, though the operation of government is the more vital field as well as the field in which outside influences are more apparent. Emphasizing the form of the Ordinance of 1787 rather than the evolution of political life under it and under later territorial frameworks, historians have tended to overstress first the liberal side of territorial government and then the autocratic side. They have overlooked the significant extent to which the territorial system, whatever its conception, figured as a channel in the large process of acculturation, transporting American ways from East to West. It performed this channeling function de-spite the motives of the framers of the Ordinance of 1787, and it may have done so the more effectively because it put Westerners under closer restraints than Jefferson had planned in 1781. The system of restraints—the authority of appointed governors, secretaries, and judges —brought with it eastern personnel and methods, and connections with eastern party systems. Jefferson himself used the territorial system as an instrument of political education and assimilation in Mississippi and Louisiana, though he had spoken of the first stage of territorial government as "a despotic oligarchy without one rational object."

On the other hand, historians of frontier justice in general have drawn less on formal than on informal sources, which tend to sustain the conventional picture of western roughness and independence. Semi-legendary frontier magistrates such as Roy Bean and Three-Legged Willie seem impregnably enshrined as western types alongside Buffalo Bill, Calamity Jane, and Black Bart. Yet between territorial judges, who usually came from the eastern bench and bar, western lawyers, who as a group were well versed in the law, the practices of the older states persisted. Territorial judges often were unpopular, but the more fundamental grievance was that there were not enough of them. Sometimes vigilantes supplanted them but chiefly when regular government had failed; and it was sometimes as significant that the vigilantes acted to protect property and to maintain some kind of due process as that they acted irregularly, or that property needed protection.

The constitutional history of all the western territories and states remains to be written. The better accounts of the processes of forming new state governments reveal a western dependence on the examples of older states that is suggestively inconsistent with the conventional view of admission to statehood as the climax of antagonism between East and West. But most of these studies are richer in detail than in analysis. There is still no western counterpart to any of the many thorough studies of institutions and functions in seventeenth-and eighteenth-century colonial government, or to Fletcher M. Green's useful survey of *Constitutional Development in the South Atlantic States.*

Constitutional innovations in the West were rare, as Turner himself noted, although in a local framework it is easy to overemphasize manhood suffrage in Vermont, woman suffrage in Wyoming, or the recall of judges in Arizona. Relative to Easterners living under older constitutions, Westerners entering the Union had unusual opportunities to make constitutional changes; but from the time when the founders of the state of Franklin turned down a more democratic system in favor of the North Carolina constitution, pioneers held to the old laws, and to the more conservative laws. John D. Hicks found few new departures, even in the "omnibus states" of 1889–1890, in a time of economic unrest. When Westerners did depart from conventional patterns, it was sometimes because eastern forms were unsuitable or meaningless (for example, a property qualification for the suffrage where either everyone had land or no one had title). Many of the innovations had come close to adoption in older states. There were few "western" reforms, in fact, that Westerners had not brought in their baggage of ideas from the East. Sometimes the raw frontier environment itself suggested so-

cial change; but on the political-constitutional plane it more often contributed to change by not including factors that had retarded or inhibited change in the older states. Frequently Westerners restricted the suffrage or the rights of Negroes by sizable majorities, while Easterners kept older restrictions only because the restrictions tended to perpetuate themselves in spite of majority opinion.

The legend of unqualified western radicalism has been especially persistent in the history of political parties, where it appears in the persons of Jefferson, Jackson, and Lincoln, to say nothing of Nathaniel Bacon or Hiram Johnson. Likewise, the Populist revolt, which so fascinated Turner and his audience in the 1890s, seems to continue to persuade us, without much more evidence, that western politics were fundamentally radical.

The history of western politics in the middle years of the nineteenth century needs further study and clarification. The figure of Lincoln himself has reached fairly sharp focus (except in some of the textbooks), but his party appears too often as the embodiment of the radical West. Yet political parties were less often media for frontier revolt against other sections than arteries by which policies and personnel moved westward. New and radical parties, unsupported by national patronage or unknown to Westerners when they were last in the East, usually took hold slowly. Beyond the Mississippi, Westerners were slow to join the Republicans, and when they did they often repudiated the radicalism of the middle-western and eastern branches of the party. Leland Stanford, campaigning in California in 1859, insisted that he preferred a white man's country, and Oregon (where, as in California, only about a third of the popular vote of 1860 was Republican) appeared with a constitution so unfriendly to Negroes and with an electorate so overwhelmingly Democratic that Congress was reluctant to grant statehood. It was not until slavery ceased to be an issue (that is, until the Democratic party was no longer the more conservative party) and until more Easterners moved West that the Far West became Republican. Westerners generally, as Josiah Royce noted of the Californians, were slow to develop new political issues.

The stories of the Federalist and Whig parties in the West of an earlier period likewise have had little interest for historians, and one may suspect that this is so because the facts do not correspond satisfactorily to the environmental-radical interpretation and do not fit easily within the conventionally local framework. We know that the Federalists openly predominated in some parts of the West, as in the Natchez area when it was first occupied. While enemies of dissident Republicans sometimes labeled them as Federalists, it is probable that under territorial government more than a few Westerners used the name Republican only because it was convenient to seem to agree with the party in power in Washington, which had a formidable weapon in the patronage and, under Jefferson, was ready to use it effectively. In a later generation, not only were some western Democrats often impressively conservative, and others of doubtful loyalty, as western Republicans had been, but the Whigs themselves were strong under their own name.

Probably no students of western society have been more active in exploring the relations of East and West than the economic historians. Western radicalism as they have pictured it came less from the physical atmosphere, whether malarial or salubrious, than in reaction to economic concentration in the West analogous to the pressure of wealth and power that simultaneously evoked radicalism in the East. The poor emigrant who found his future on the frontier is an authentic figure, but Paul W. Gates has shown the prevalence of tenancy in the Old Northwest, and Fred A. Shannon has footnoted the darkest pictures of Hamlin Garland, all but proving that west of the Missouri River there could be no westward movement at all, in the traditional sense.

The economic history of even the preagricultural frontiers, once a pageant of individual adventure, is coming to rest on the cold facts of investment capital. Even in the early stages, the frontier invited collective exploitation from without, while it disposed frontiersmen to undertake collective action to meet new problems that put too much strain on individual effort. Because large-sized economic units or aggregations were necessary in the West, the West sometimes assumed a more capitalistic shape than the East. It may have retained it more securely because (at least before the 1890s) there was no self-conscious western proletariat to resist frontier capitalism. The masses might not acquire property of their own, but they believed that they might; and in any event the majority of Westerners, scattered and preoccupied with individual tasks and aspirations, could not effectively resist the capitalist or eastern orientation of western economic life. "The real peculiarity of our present Pacific civilization," said *Overland,* "is that it is, perhaps, the most completely realized embodiment of the purely commercial civilization on the face of the earth." Yet romantic biases still dictate the proportions of much of our western economic history. We still know the homesteader better than the landlord, the railroad builder better than the railroad operator. The trapper, the prospector, and the cowboy, moving picturesquely over a background of clean air and great distances, hold us more than the tycoons and corporations that dominated them and the Rocky Mountain country.

The historian's selection of picaresque and romantic characters is particularly clear in most western social history. The indolent backwoodsman—some variant of the Boone stereotype, ever retreating before civilization—typifies frontier degradation. "Is it not time," Frederick Law Olmsted asked in 1859, that "the people of the Free West were delivered from the vague reputation of bad temper, recklessness, and lawlessness, under which they suffer?" The general impression of lawless violence in the West, he contended, was "based upon, and entirely sustained by, occurrences which are peculiar to the frontier of the Slave States." Yet the legend prevailed, and today some southern historians insist that Olmsted actually described the West rather than the South when he painted his most unattractive pictures of slaveholding society, and quote his words to illustrate the view of the West that he had rejected.

Local foreign groups have loomed over-large, on the other hand, whether because they were. colorful or because they represented a more indigenous and environmental cultural ingredient than the Americans who moved in from the East. The role of Spanish culture in the Southwest has been exaggerated from the day of Helen Hunt Jackson and the Ramona legend to the day of the latest real estate speculator who manufactures Spanish-sounding place names. Actually the native Spanish and Mexican elements in many parts of the West—particularly California, where they are most revered today—were small and uninfluential, often fairly recent arrivals themselves; the typical American settler was ignorant of their language and despised their institutions.

English-speaking aristocracies meanwhile have been less prominent in books on the West. In neglecting prosperous and conservative transplanted elements in the pioneer Southwest, many historians have submitted to a stereotype as readily as those who describe southern antebellum society and slavery entirely from the records and prejudices of the great planters and neglect the yeoman farmers. Yet students of the southern frontier have been particularly successful in tracing continuity in social institutions and social stratification.

The educated well-to-do families of the Frankfort area kept up "the ancient customs and fashions of the English," recalled the Reverend James B. Finley. These new planters may have seemed upstarts to their counterparts in the eastern states, who had forgotten their own pioneer past, but often they were equally devoted to tradition. Farther west, though distances from the East were greater, improved transportation and new riches sustained even larger aristocracies. The flourishing commerce of cities such as New Orleans and St. Louis brought in scores of professional businessmen; the mines and cattle ranches of the Far West drew on all classes of society, Easterners becoming more prominent than in the older West. "You will often find some graduate of Yale 'bull-whacking' his own team from the river to the mines, looking as if he had seldom seen soap and water," reported a traveler from Colorado. There were enough gentleman ranchers and miners, rich men with weak lungs, officeholders and lawyers to add substantial cultural leavening, in a West that was quick to demand schools, colleges, and grand opera. That aristocracies existed is unmistakable, but they are so new as subjects of serious historical study that historians have not sufficiently appraised their role in the West or compared them with aristocracies in the East. We know too little about the structure of western society to be sure that it behaved conservatively on occasion because the aristocrats had overawed it or because aristocratic oppression was too slight to arouse sharp class consciousness, because monopoly was too incomplete to make a farce of the western habit of measuring success by material standards. . . .

An appraisal of western conservatism and continuity, however, must leave ample room for qualification, and not merely exchange new narrowness for old. It would be as easy to exaggerate conservatism in the 1950s as it was to exaggerate radicalism in the 1890s. Sharp distinctions between liberal and conservative factors are sure to be artificial, and they are especially suspect in the history of a transplanted society. In part the conservative West of the nineteenth century was the copy of the East that it tried to be. It contained hierarchies of culture, wealth, and influence in which the upper classes were small but influential beyond their size; it clung to traditional institutional forms and social practices; and it hungered after intellectual and social contact and parity with the East. A large part of western opportunity was the opportunity to imitate an older society. At the same time, realization tended to fall short of aspiration; and both innovations and transplantations were often unfinished business, forced to give priority to the more pressing problems of subsistence. Thus neither the radical nor the conservative could even try to go so far as he might wish to go. A western aristocracy was likely to be newer and more mobile than its counterpart in the East, and generally innocent of any body of ideas or sense of social responsibility comparable to the constructive political philosophy of a John Adams or a Henry L. Stimson. Much western conservatism might as well be called materialism. Yet some such differences were only relative. To an Englishman, the ascent of the Schoenberg-Belmont family within two generations in New York might seem only somewhat less surprising than the ascent and descent of the Tabor family within two decades in Colorado.

The historian of the Pacific Coast states, as of any of the newer wests, must guard especially against forcing the history of the whole West into a new pattern, though thus far much popular Pacific Coast history simply dresses Daniel Boone in *chaparajos* and puts the Mississippi River toughs on horseback. The dude ranch country of the Rocky Mountains may too readily conclude that it is the most western part of the West, as if Wall Street ruled only in the shadows of the skyscrapers; West Texas may too readily conclude that it comprises all of America. But the coast began by being closer to the East than the interior was; and if San Francisco brings the aspirations of the West to focus, so that one cannot understand the Nevada desert without knowing also "the city," the city alone tells little of the desert to one who has not gone there.

Two generations after Turner set forth his environmental interpretation of the American West, it seems to rest more on tradition than on the testimony of recent events. As we move away from his time, our own time alerts us to continuity and conservatism, among other schemes. The volume of research on the more recent West increases, even while the pioneer period dominates most courses and textbooks on the history of the West and many western history research libraries. The historian cannot easily ignore the challenge to explain this new present in which he lives and works, a present in which West and East are visibly more alike than they were in Turner's day. Some of Turner's critics, on the other hand, have been moved too much by the atmosphere of their own time and of their own section, and have, in effect, condemned the nineteenth-century West because it is not the twentieth-century East. Both they and those Westerners who achieve a new antiquarianism in a narrow treatment of recent events pass by the larger opportunities of western history.

It may be that the greater stimulus to western history-writing could come from other fields. It would be useful, for instance, for western historians, who in a large sense are colonial historians, to look more closely at our colonial roots. As a group, colonial historians have been far more successful than the Westerners in integrating their story into large re-

gional patterns and in exploring institutions and ideas. The western historian might be more critical of his sources and his premises if he had not tended to drift so far into intellectual isolation from his colleagues. Cultivating selected furrows in a separate patch, he confirms his isolation by retaining to an unusual degree an earlier generation's faith in accumulated information, even though his field is one whose personnel and specific events are so little known that he has an unusual obligation to present them in large patterns and attractive style. Correspondingly, some of the most thoughtful contributions to western history have seemed to be, if not products of intellectual hybridization, at least the work of men who ignore the orthodox limitations of the western historian.

If there is an answer to the complaint against the restricted outlook of western historians, it is not likely to be found in decrying Turner's mistakes and the inspiration of his time, nor in depreciating the reverence that he still commands. It would be no solution to turn western history over to economists, political scientists, and others not conversant with the massive literature of the field, though when they have tried their hand at it as critics of Turner some of them have done embarrassingly well, and Turner's defenders have not clearly done better in the argument. Rather the trouble with western history may be that we are not enough like Turner in his larger qualities: his concern for both analysis and synthesis, his effective English style, and the keenness of his mind. Turner advocated a radical-environmental approach, but it is clear enough from what he said about other forces in the West, including eastern forces, that he did not hold to that approach alone. The prophet was less orthodox than the priesthood. He was a good salesman, and he had other errors to combat in his time, by over-emphasis if necessary. He showed clearly where his preference lay between the antiquarians and those who considered western history "in its relations to world-history, not in the spirit of the local his-torian," appreciating that they were "de-scribing a phase in the general move-ment of civilization." He taught courses in national as well as regional history; and his students ranged widely into other fields and other interpretations, as he had done in his own university studies and teaching.

Turner never suggested that pioneering was the only force shaping the American character. His disciples, however, were sometimes less cautious. Hence modern social scientists, when advancing or defending other explanations for the distinctiveness of American traits, feel called upon to tilt with the Turnerians and prove the superiority of their own interpretation over that of the frontier school. One group of scholars, led by the historian George W. Pierson and the demographer Everett S. Lee, have argued that the excessive mobility of the people of the United States accounts for many of the characteristics usually associated with pioneering. EVERETT S. LEE (1919–   ) of the department of sociology of the University of Pennsylvania has penned an effective argument in support of what Pierson calls the M-Factor in American history.*

Mobility a Strong Influence

In a meeting at the Chicago World's Fair in 1893, Frederick Jackson Turner, then a young man of 32, read a paper entitled "The Significance of the Frontier in American History," doubtless the most influential paper ever presented before a congress of historians. According to Riegel, "The rapid and almost complete acceptance of Turnerian ideas soon produced a flood of references by historians, sociologists, novelists, playwrights, and in fact by almost anyone sufficiently literate to put pen on paper. The historic Turner essay seemed to rate only slightly lower in the popular estimation than the Bible, the Constitution, and the Declaration of Independence." Franklin Delano Roosevelt drew upon it to justify the ways of the New Deal. Said he: "Equality of opportunity as we have known it no longer exists. . . . Our last frontier has long since been reached, and there is practically no more free land. . . . There is no safety valve in the form of a Western prairie to which those thrown out of work by the Eastern economic machines can go for a new start. . . ."

Part of the appeal of the Turner thesis was its boldness and simplicity. In his own words, "The existence of an area of free land, its continuous recession, and the advance of American settlement west-

* Everett S. Lee, "The Turner Thesis Re-examined," *American Quarterly*, vol. 13 (Spring 1961), pp. 77–87. Printed without footnotes by permission of Everett S. Lee and the editor of the *American Quarterly*.

ward, explain American development." It was the free lands of the West that constituted a safety valve for discontented Eastern masses and furnished the nationalizing impulses that bound the loose confederation of states into a strong central government. Even more important, it was "to the frontier the American intellect owes its striking characteristics. That coarseness and strength combined with acuteness and inquisitiveness; that practical, inventive turn of mind, quick to find expedients; that masterful grasp of material things, lacking in the artistic but powerful to effect great ends; that restless, nervous energy; that dominant individualism, working for good and for evil, and withal that buoyancy and exuberance which comes with freedom— these are traits of the frontier." Regretfully Turner noted at the conclusion of his essay that "The frontier is gone, and with its going has closed the first period of American history."

Most of us are now several generations removed from our pioneer forebears, if indeed we had any, and most of us have been rendered cautious by the reception accorded more recent monistic explanations of national character. It now seems obvious that the Turner thesis is too simple an explanation for such complexities as American democracy and American character, so after forty years of general and enthusiastic acceptance it is now the fashion to attack Turner's propositions. It can fairly be said that the supporting evidence was meager and that the thesis was not so much proved as reiterated. Nevertheless, there is great intuitive appeal in this theory, and few are willing to abandon it entirely.

In part, the Turner thesis still commands credence because of the admittedly crucial importance of vast areas of free land during the formative period of American democracy, but another reason for its appeal is that Turner, in emphasizing the frontier, was developing a special case of a more general theory of migration. Most of the effects, desirable and undesirable, that were attributed by Turner to the frontier can, with equal or better logic, be attributed to migration, and in addition, the migration theory does not collapse or depend upon tradition for its maintenance after the frontier is gone. It is not meant by this to substitute one monistic explanation of American development for another. The point is that migration has been a force of greatest moment in American civilization, and that from the magnitude and character of migration within this country certain consequences logically follow. And yet these in turn reinforce the tendency to migrate, so that when we try to arrive at cause and effect we are caught in a never ending circle in which the apparent effects viewed in a different way seem to have produced the very phenomena we first accounted as causes. It is therefore not maintained, paraphrasing Turner, that migration explains American civilization. It certainly does not, but that it was and is a major force in the development of American civilization and in the shaping of American character hardly anyone will deny. The magnitude and uniqueness of internal migration in the United States are, however, not generally realized, and research on migration differentials is only beginning to reveal the concomitants of continual movement from place to place.

In America we can say that migration is a part of our way of life. We are all but a few generations removed from our immigrant ancestors, whether they landed at Plymouth Rock or Ellis Island. Within our country, migration is of such scale as to astound foreign observers. In recent years one in each five persons moved from one house to another in each twelve-month period, one in fourteen migrated from one county to another, and one in thirty from one state to another. These are crude figures for both sexes and all ages. At the age of maximum migration, 20-24, one in six males moved from one county to another, and one in ten shifted state of residence. Over twenty percent of the native population lives outside the state of birth, but again this figure is a weighted average for all ages and makes the incidence of interstate migration seem smaller than it is, since at ages fifty and thereafter nearly two out of five native Americans have set up residence outside the state of birth. Migration of this order has been the rule rather than the exception in American history, and calculations made independently by Henry S. Shyrock and myself indicate that the present high level of interstate migration has existed since at least 1850.

Moreover the figures cited are underestimates. They all relate to net migrants, those persons who moved during a given period and who had not died nor returned to the county or state of birth. It is well known that net internal migration is generally but a small residue left from the interplay of much larger streams of in- and out-migration. Who has not known the migrant who returned from afar to his place of origin, or the person who is constantly moving from one place to another? Those of us who are not migrants have many contacts with such persons, some from distant states. There is probably no community of any size which is so isolated that it has not felt the impact of migration, either from the loss of its members, or from the entrance of persons from other communities, or almost invariably, from both. We are indeed a nation of migrants and we always have been.

Had our ancestors not been willing migrants and were we as a people not willing to pull up stakes to strike out for greener pastures, American economic development would have been seriously retarded and could not operate with its present efficiency. Modern capitalism demands the quick exploitation of new resources and the abandonment of those which no longer pay well. Here new resources, wherever located, can draw upon a large and almost instantaneous labor supply, and workers do not wait for local resources to be exhausted before moving elsewhere in desperation. The mushrooming mining towns of the West in the 1850s and 1860s have their modern counterparts in the newly established cities that center around defense industries. The exodus of farmers from the rocky slopes of New England into western New York and Ohio has been exceeded in magnitude by the desertion of the dust bowl for California and the Northwest. Contrast this situation with that which is found in some other countries where a labor surplus may exist in a community ten miles from one in which there is a labor shortage, and yet the government finds it hard to persuade unemployed workers to make the short move toward ready employment.

In this connection, it should be pointed out that the true safety valve was not the frontier, even before its alleged disappearance about 1890: it was migration, sometimes to the frontier it is true, sometimes to better farming lands far behind the frontier, but more often it was from the farm to the city. Migration to the city has almost always exceeded the movement to the frontier, and in recent years the migration to Turner's West, however defined, has been to the city rather than to open country. The city has more often been an outlet for the underemployed of rural areas than the farm a haven for the unemployed workers in Eastern industries.

We now know that migrants are not a cross section of the general population. Internal migration as well as external migration is selective, especially for young adults in the ages of greatest productivity and also of greatest reproductivity. The characteristics of migrants between states are somewhat similar to those of migrants from abroad in the days of peak immigration. Males predominate and they are concentrated at ages 20 to 30. Migrants are better educated than nonmigrants, and the highest migration rates are for those at the top of the occupational ladder. The fragmentary studies that exist even suggest that migrants are more intelligent than nonmigrants.

In addition to being young, migrants are likely to be single or in the early stages of family formation. As size of family increases, even when age of head is held constant, there is a decrease in migration. With migration recognized as a part of the way of life, an extra premium is placed upon family limitation and it may be suggested that students who are puzzled by the early fall in the birth rate in the United States, prior even to that in France, consider migration as a predisposing factor. More important, perhaps, than the stimulus to family limitation is the breakdown of the *grossfamilie* system with its encompassed generations and its extension of the privileges and obligations of kinship to cousins of remote degree. By migrating from his clan the individual removes himself from

its control and from its protection. Were it not that a highly developed sense of individualism prompted his move in the first place, it would be necessary to acquire it. He and his family become a self-supporting and, to some degree, a self-sufficient little unit. Since he must fight his own battles and provide his own subsistence without the support of his clan he becomes impatient with the demands of distant relatives upon him.

In some persons individualism may manifest itself, as in Turner's frontiersman, in truculence and uncouthness, but most migrants find that a premium is placed upon the ability to adjust to new situations and new people. They learn the value of outward conformity and may come to place great value upon it. They make acquaintances easily—in short, they exhibit many of the characteristics of today's "organization man," and I wonder if the attributes of this gentleman are not largely those in which generations of Americans have been schooled. Incidentally, the "organization man" is likely to be exceptionally migratory because of the practice of large companies of regularly transferring officials from plant to plant or from branch to branch.

A highly mobile population is not one in which an hereditary elite is likely to develop. Migration diminishes the value of blood ties and the possession of a distinguished name may come to mean little. In Massachusetts and South Carolina Adams and Pinckney may be names to conjure with, but what do they mean in Brooklyn and Whisky Gulch? A different set of values distinguishes the mobile from the static society. Land ownership, for example, as a mark of status gives way to more transportable items, among which ability and money are prominent.

It is hardly necessary to note that in the long run nationalism is promoted by interstate migration. Turner, himself, remarked that "Nothing works for nationalism like intercourse within the nation" and that "mobility of population is death to localism." The migrant from Alabama to Detroit is likely to waver in his devotion to state's rights, and the northern metropolis which acquires the product of a South Carolina public school for Negroes is led to wonder whether that state can be entrusted with so important a function as education. Not only does migration promote nationalism and lessen the attachment to a state or locality but it also serves to encourage the extension of the functions of national government into areas once reserved for the states.

With our set of values most of the things we have associated with migration seem desirable. Individualism and equalitarianism are usually associated with democracy, and the creation of a strong central government seems necessary for survival. But tendencies toward conformity and the extension of federal functions may be disturbing. Let us now consider some of the less desirable aspects of migration.

In studying one of our most migratory groups, young executives, researchers noted that though superficial friendships are made readily, there was reluctance to form deep attachments with emotional ties and mutual obligations, partly because they would be interrupted by migration. It would seem that an almost inevitable result of migration with its severing of friendships is the focusing of emotional relationships inward to the immediate family with perhaps too much expected of each member.

Such tensions, if they exist, are minor in comparison with those which result from unsuccessful efforts to adjust or conform, or from rebellion. It is now evident that rates of admission to mental hospitals are much higher for migrants than of nonmigrants and, while this may be true in part because of selection for disease-prone individuals as migrants, the struggle with the changing environment must also play a part. Often the migrant does not understand the reasons for doing things in a particular way in a new community. For example, the detailed sanitary regulations of the northern city may be looked upon as restrictions of freedom by a migrant from the rural South. With rapidly shifting populations, custom cannot be depended upon for controls which are automatically effective in static societies, and, since education is too slow and too costly, laws are proliferated.

Migration often breeds carelessness as to immediate surroundings. Few people hope to remain in the slums and not many young people expect to. If surroundings become too bad the quickest and easiest remedy is migration. Local reform movements are hampered and cities remain "corrupt and contented" partly because the natural leaders move to the suburbs. Newcomers are not always aware of the true nature of civic problems and may be tempted by the immediate favors of the political boss to vote against long-range improvements. And, when the newcomer realizes what the situation is, it is much easier to migrate than to attempt reform.

Migrants are likely to meet their numerous new situations with temporary expedients at the expense of long-run solutions. The most characteristic of American philosophies, pragmatism, which stresses continuous short-term ad-

justments in the conviction that whatever works is best, is a typically migrant
philosophy. If, in the long run, we are
not dead, we may at least be somewhere
else. This carries over into a general
emphasis on immediate practicality at
the cost of interest in philosophical questions. Perhaps our national bias against
basic science or "nonpaying" research is
partly due to the spatial restlessness of
the American people.

Also, the American penchant for change
for change's sake may be associated with
our geographic mobility. Migration has
been phenomenally successful for Americans. The immigrants from abroad did
find superior economic opportunities,
and if they were fleeing oppression they
found freedom. Within our country the
major flows of migration have been from
areas of lower to higher economic returns, or from areas in which the amenities were less developed to those in
which they were better developed. The
natural interpretation by the migrant is
that migration has been a good thing;
having done it once he is willing to do it
again if another area looks more attractive. This attitude he imparts to his
children and to nonmigrants with whom

he comes in contact. In itself, migration
is one of the most drastic social changes;
if this is so generally successful, why not
other types of change?

In conclusion, it is again stated that
no attempt is made to explain American
democracy or American character. It is
maintained, however, that from a psycho-
logical and sociological, as well as from
an economic, point of view, migration is
one of the most important factors in
American civilization. There are few
characteristics which are shared by so
many Americans as migrant status and
spatial movement has correlates which
are both good and bad. They have not,
however, been thoroughly studied. Sixty
years ago Turner's thesis set off a round
of the most productive studies in American history. A case can be made that his
frontier theory is a special case of an as
yet undeveloped migration theory. The
tools and the data are now available for
extensive research on the effects of migration, and it is hoped that historians and
sociologists will now begin to study migration in the larger context of its effect
upon the development of the American
people.

If the migratory instinct has been assigned responsibility for many of the traits that distinguish Americans, so has the abundance of natural resources with which the United States is blessed. DAVID M. POTTER (1910–   ), Coe Professor of History at Stanford University, holds that the American character is partially the product of the continuing exploitation of these resources, creating as they have a "people of plenty." To this, Turnerians answer that had there been no frontier, the resources would have been so depleted by prior generations that the nation's abundance would have been far less. They also insist that modern mobility is traceable to the habit of moving about, which was bred into the people by the pioneering experience. Whatever the truth, Potter has advanced a thoughtful concept and has quarreled vigorously with the Turnerians in so doing.*

The Role of Abundance

Such, then, were the main elements of the frontier hypothesis, as Turner developed it: West of the Alleghenies lay a vast expanse of fertile and unsettled land which became available almost free to those who would cultivate it. Across this area, a frontier or edge of settlement pushed steadily west, and along this frontier individuals who had advanced ahead of society's usual institutional controls accepted a lowering of standards at the time for the sake of progress in the future. Constantly repeating over again a democratic experience, they reinforced the national democratic tradition. All these conditions, of course, influenced the mental traits of those who were directly or indirectly involved in the process, and especially their nationalism, their democracy, and their individualism were stimulated. Certain other qualities—a coarseness, combined with a strength, a practicality and materialism of mind, a restless energy, and a measure of buoyancy or exuberance—were all traceable to this frontier influence.

With this outline of the frontier hypothesis in mind, we can now revert to the question: To what extent was the frontier merely the context in which abundance occurred? To what extent does it explain developments which the

* David M. Potter, *People of Plenty: Economic Abundance and the American Character* (Chicago, University of Chicago Press, 1954), pp. 154–160. Reprinted by permission of David M. Potter and the University of Chicago Press.

concept of abundance alone could not explain?

At times Turner himself seemed almost to equate the frontier with abundance, as, for instance, when he said, "These free lands promoted individualism, economic equality, freedom to rise, democracy." It is probably valid to criticize him for this. But if there was a fallacy in his failure to distinguish between these coinciding factors and his consequent practice of treating qualities which were intrinsically derived from abundance as if they were distinctive to the frontier, it would be the same fallacy in reverse to treat qualities which were intrinsically frontier qualities as if they were attributable to abundance. Bearing this caveat in mind, we can hardly deny that there were a number of influences which were peculiar to the frontier or to abundance in its distinctive frontier form and which did not operate outside the frontier phase. For instance, the pioneer's necessity of submitting to hardships and low living standards as the price of higher standards later must certainly have stimulated his optimism and his belief in progress. Similarly, one can hardly doubt that the mingling of peoples on the frontier and their urgent need for federal legislative measures must have stimulated the growth of nationalism just as Turner said. And again, at an even deeper level, it is hard to doubt that the frontier projection of the individual ahead of society and the self-sufficing way of life on the edge of settlement must have greatly stimulated American individualism.

But even to say that Turner was right in all these matters is not to say that he took a comprehensive view of the American experience. By confining his explanation of Americanism to the conditions of the pioneer stage of our development, he placed himself in the position of implying that nothing distinctively American would be left, except as a residue, after the pioneer stage had been passed. By limiting his recognition of abundance to its appearance in the form of free land, he limited his recognition of successive American democratic readjustments to the successive settlement of new areas of free land, and thus he cut himself off from a recognition of the adjustments to technological advance, to urban growth, and to the higher standard of living, all of which have contributed quite as much as the frontier to the fluidity and facility for change in American life. Further, by failing to recognize that the frontier was only one form in which America offered abundance, he cut himself off from an insight into the fact that other forms of abundance had superseded the frontier even before the supply of free land had been exhausted, with the result that it was not really the end of free land but rather the substitution of new forms of economic activity which terminated the frontier phase of our history.

Perhaps it may be in order to say a few words more about each of these points. In the first place, then, by making the frontier the one great hopeful factor in our experience, Turner gave us every cause to feel alarm and pessimism about the conditions that would follow the disappearance of the frontier. As he himself expressed it, "since the days when the fleet of Columbus sailed into the waters of the New World, America has been another name for opportunity. . . . He would be a rash prophet who should assert that the expansive character of American life has now entirely ceased. Movement has been its dominant fact, and, unless this training has no effect upon a people, the American energy will continually demand a wider field for its exercise. But never again will such gifts of free land offer themselves. . . . Now, four centuries from the discovery of America, at the end of a hundred years of life under the Constitution, the frontier has gone, and with its going has closed the first period of American history."

The tone of foreboding in this statement is easily transformed into a defeatist lament or into a conviction that, without the frontier, freedom and opportunity are endangered. To take but one of a good many possible illustrations, Governor Philip La Follette, in his message to the Wisconsin legislature in 1931, observed that "in the days of our pioneer fathers, the free land of the frontier gave this guarantee of freedom and opportunity," but that no such natural safeguard remained in operation after the passing of the frontier.

Some years ago Dixon Ryan Fox pointed out this defeatist corollary of the frontier hypothesis and suggested that broader definition of a frontier which I have already mentioned—namely, "the edge of the unused." This would imply, of course, that science has its frontiers, industry its frontiers, technology its frontiers, and that so long as Americans can advance their standards of living and maintain the fluidity of their lives and their capacity for change along these frontiers, the disappearance of the agrarian frontier is not at all critical. In terms of abundance, Turner was correct in saying, "Never again will such gifts of free land offer themselves," but his implication that nature would never again offer such bounty is open to challenge, for the frontiers of industry, of invention, and of engineering have continued to bring into play new resources quite as rich as the unbroken sod of the western frontier.

A second point which I believe Turner's agrarian orientation caused him to overlook was the broad variety of factors which have worked to cause unceasing change and development in America and thereby have conditioned the American to a habit of constant adjustment, constant adaptation to new circumstances, and constant readiness to accept or experiment with what is new. It was "to the frontier" that he attributed "that practical inventive turn of mind, quick to find expedients," to it that he credited the fact that Americans were "compelled to adapt themselves to the changes of an expanding people." But clearly it is not "the simplicity of primitive society" which requires new expedients and inventive ability; on the contrary, primitive society was highly repetitive in its patterns and demanded stamina more than talent for innovation; it was an increasingly complex society of rapid technological change, far away from the frontier, which demanded range and flexibility of adjustment. No amount of concentration upon the frontier will give us an awareness of the way in which the American home has been readjusted to the use first of gas and later of electricity; of the way in which American business has been readjusted to the typewriter and the comptometer; of the way in which American communication has been adjusted to the telegraph, the telephone, the radio, and even the motion picture; and of the way in which the American community has been readjusted to the railroad, the streetcar, and the automobile. One has only to compare an old, preautomobile city, like Boston, with a new, postautomobile city, like Houston, Texas, with its supermarkets, its drive-in restaurants, and its other facilities for automotive living, to appreciate that this is true. Are not these constant changes more important in maintaining the fluidity of American life, in perpetuating the habit of expecting something different, than any number of successive removals to new areas of free land?

A third and final aspect in which the agrarian perspective proved too limiting is in the fact that Turner did not recognize that the attraction of the frontier was simply as the most accessible form of abundance, and therefore he could not conceive that other forms of abundance might replace it as the lodestone to which the needle of American aspirations would point. To him the frontier remained the polar force until it was exhausted; America must turn to second-best resources after this unparalled opportunity of the frontier had passed. Yet, in fact, what happened was that, as early as the mid-century, if not earlier, American industrial growth, relying upon the use of other forms of abundance than soil fertility, began to compete with the frontier in the opportunities which it offered, and the migration of Americans began to point to the cities rather than to the West. Later, this same industrial growth provided a general standard of living so high that people were no longer willing to abandon it for the sake of what the frontier promised. This can be stated almost in the terms of a formula: The frontier, with its necessity for some reduction of living standards, could at-

tract people from settled areas so long as the existing standards in those areas did not exceed a certain maximum (people would accept a certain unfavorable differential in their current standards for the sake of potential gain). But when existing city standards exceeded this maximum, when the differential became too great, people would no longer accept it even for all the future rewards that the frontier might promise. To leave a primitive agrarian community and settle in primitive agrarian isolation was one thing, but to leave refrigeration, electric lighting, running water, hospitals, motion pictures, and access to highways was another, and, as these amenities and others like them were introduced, the frontier distinctly lost the universality of its lure. As George W. Pierson says, "When cars, movies, and radios become essentials of the accepted standard of living, subsistence farming is repugnant even to the starving. Measured, therefore, against this concept of a changing fashion or standard of living, it may be suggested that the lure of the land began in Tudor England before there was any available, and ceased in the United States before the available supply gave out." In short, the frontier ceased to operate as a major force in American history not when it disappeared—not when the superintendent of the census abandoned the attempt to map a frontier boundary—but when the primary means of access to abundance passed from the frontier to other focuses in American life.

No summary of the arguments against the frontier thesis is more comprehensive than that prepared by RICHARD HOFSTADTER (1916–   ), Columbia University historian, in 1949, as the period of attack on the hypothesis was drawing to a close. Hofstadter can be classed as a student of the American mind rather than as a student of the American frontier. The fresh interpretations of the past contained in such books as *The American Political Tradition* and *The Age of Reform* have embroiled him in controversy and marked him as one of the most original thinkers in the field of American history. While he has drawn upon the writings of other critics in the essay that follows, he has added his own insights as well.*

The Thesis Disputed

American historical writing in the past century has produced two major theories or models of understanding, the economic interpretation of politics associated with Charles A. Beard, and the frontier interpretation of American development identified with Frederick Jackson Turner. Both views have had a pervasive influence upon American thinking, but Beard himself felt that Turner's original essay on the frontier had "a more profound influence on thought about American history than any other essay or volume ever written on the subject." It is the frontier thesis that has embodied the predominant American view of the American past.

Turner wrote his memorable essay, "The Significance of the Frontier in American History," during that period of growing tension between the Eastern and Western United States which culminated in the Bryan campaign of 1896. An expression of rising Western self-consciousness, Turner's thesis was meant to challenge the dominant academic school of Eastern historians then led by his former teacher, Herbert Baxter Adams. The members of this school concerned themselves chiefly with the development of American political institutions. Their controlling assumption was that American democracy and local self-government had come, by way of England, from remote Anglo-Saxon political institutions like the Witanagemot, which could be traced back to the forests of Germany. Under the sway of Darwinian evolutionism, they followed the genetic method with the passion of zealots and doctrinaires; they attributed to political institutions a kind of self-contained and self-determining cycle of growth comparable to that of a living organism.

Like the Easterners, Turner was an evolutionist concerned primarily with political forms. But in contrast to the Adams school, with its reliance upon racial heredity and self-determined growth, Turner looked for the influence of environment. In his opinion, the Adams school was paying far too much attention to the European "germs" of American institutions, and far too little to the American soil in which these "germs" had grown. It was not the self-unfolding of imported institutions, but rather the events that took place on native grounds, that decided the course of American development. The unique and distinguishing elements of American history could be found on the American scene in the shape of the frontier and free land. "The existence of an area of free land, its continuous recession, and the advance of American settlement westward explain American development."

American evolution, Turner believed, had been a repeated return to primitive conditions on a continually receding frontier line, a constant repetition of development from simple conditions to a complex society. From this perennial rebirth and fluidity of American life, and from its continual re-exposure to the simplicity of primitive society, had come the forces dominant in the American character. And as the frontier advanced, society moved steadily away from Euro-

pean influences, grew steadily on distinctive American lines. To study this advance and the men who had been fashioned by it was "to study the really American part of our history."

Of all the effects of the frontier, the most important was that it promoted democracy and individualism. So long as free land existed, there was always opportunity for a man to acquire a competency, and economic power secured political power. Each succeeding frontier furnished "a new field of opportunity, a gate of escape from the bondage of the past." The lack of binding tradition and organized restraints promoted a distinctively American passion for individual freedom, antipathy to direct control from outside, aggressive self-interest, and intolerance of education and administrative experience. But by the year 1890, this process had come to an end; the frontier, the hither edge of unsettled land, no longer existed, and with its passing the first epoch of American history had closed. . . .

The initial plausibility of the Turner thesis lies in the patent fact that no nation could spend more than a century developing an immense continental empire without being deeply affected by it. Few critics question the great importance of the inland empire, or that Turner originally performed a service for historical writing by directing attention to it. Many accept Turner's emphasis on the frontier as one of several valid but limited perspectives on American history. But it has been forcefully denied that the frontier deserves any special pre-eminence among several major factors in "explaining" American development. The question has also been raised (and frequently answered in the negative) whether Turner analyzed the frontier process itself clearly or correctly.

It became plain, as new thought and research was brought to bear upon the problem, that the frontier theory, as an analytic device, was a blunt instrument. The terms with which the Turnerians dealt—the frontier, the West, individualism, the American character—were vague at the outset, and as the Turnerian exposition developed, they did not receive increasingly sharp definition. Precisely because Turner defined the frontier so loosely ("the term," he said, "is an elastic one"), he could claim so much for it. At times he referred to the frontier literally as the edge of the settled territory having a population density of two to the square mile. But frequently he identified "the frontier" and "the West," so that areas actually long settled could be referred to as frontier. At times he spoke of both the "frontier" and the "West" not as places or areas, but as a social process: "The West, at bottom, is a form of society rather than an area." When this definition is followed to its logical conclusion, the development of American society is "explained" by "a form of society"— certainly a barren tautology. Again, at times Turner assimilated such natural resources as coal, oil, timber, to the idea of "the West"; in this way the truism that natural wealth has an important bearing upon a nation's development and characteristics was subtly absorbed into the mystique of the frontier and took on the guise of a major insight.

However, the central weakness of Turner's thesis was in ·its intellectual isolationism. Having committed himself to an initial overemphasis on the uniqueness of the historical development of the United States, Turner compounded the error by overemphasizing the frontier as a factor in this development. The obsession with uniqueness, the subtly demagogic stress on "the truly American part of our history," diverted the attention of historical scholarship from the possibilities of comparative social history; it offered no opportunity to explain why so many features of American development—for example, the rise of democracy in the nineteenth century—were parallel to changes in countries that did not have a contiguous frontier. Historians were encouraged to omit a host of basic influences common to both American and Western European development—the influence of Protestantism and the Protestant ethic, the inheritance from English republicanism, the growth of industrialism and urbanism. More than this, factors outside the frontier process that contributed to the singularity of American history were skipped over: the peculiar American federal structure, the slave system and the Southern caste complex, immigration and ethnic heterogeneity, the unusually capitalistic and speculative character of American agriculture, the American inheritance of *laissez faire*. The interpretation seems particularly weak for the corporate-industrial phase of American history that followed the Civil War. Indeed, if the historian's range of vision had to be limited to one explanatory idea, as it fortunately does not, one could easily argue that the business corporation was the dominant dynamic factor in American development during this period.

As a form of geographical determinism, the frontier interpretation is vulnerable on still another ground. If the frontier alone was a self-sufficient source of democracy and individualism, whatever the institutions and ideas the frontiersmen brought with them, frontiers elsewhere ought to have had a similar effect. The early frontier of seignorial French Canada, the South American frontier, and the Siberian frontier should have fostered democracy and individualism. The frontier should have forged the same kind of democracy when planters came to Mississippi as when yeomen farmers came to Illinois. Turner's dictum, "American democracy came out of the American forest," proved to be a questionable improvement upon the notion of his predecessors that it came out of the German forest. Plainly the whole complex of institutions, habits and ideas that men brought to the frontier was left out of his formula, and it was these things, not bare geography, that had been decisive. Turner's analysis, as George Warren Pierson aptly put it, hung too much on real estate, not enough on a state of mind.

If American democracy originated on the frontier or in the West, it ought to be possible to trace successive waves of democratic sentiment and practice from West to East. But when the periods of democractic advance are examined, no such process can be found. After almost two centuries of life under frontier conditions in colonial America, democracy had made little headway; society was still highly stratified and the suffrage was restricted. The American Revolution gave a considerable impetus to dêmocratic developments, but it is not easy to assign any priority in the Revolution to the Western or frontier population. Eastern merchants took a notable part in the pre-Revolutionary agitation—as did urban mobs and Eastern farmers, who also contributed much to the fighting. The ideas that were used to justify the Revolution and later adapted to the democratic cause were not generated in the wilds around Kaskaskia, but derived from the English republicanism of the seventeenth century—notably, of course, from Locke.

Both great periods of the upsurge of democracy in nineteenth-century America, the Jeffersonian and the Jacksonian, are far more intelligible in terms of social classes than of the East or the West, if only because both had so much strength in Eastern and urban areas. Jeffersonianism which was strong among seaboard slaveholders and in many of the towns, is somewhat more comprehensible as a movement of agrarians against capitalists, than as a movement of the frontier against the East. The age of Jackson has been held up more than any other as an example of the democratic spirit of the frontier in action. Yet Arthur M. Schlesinger, Jr.'s recent study of that era does not employ the frontier thesis, and it is highly successful in asserting the crucial role of Eastern Jacksonians. With the exception of a few scattered local areas, many of which were in the West, Jackson swept the country when he was elected in 1828, and Jacksonian democracy can best be understood as a nationwide movement, supported by parts of the planting, farming, laboring and entrepreneurial classes.

It may be conceded to the Turnerians that the West occassionally gave democratic ideas an especially favorable area for operation—but it should be conceded in return that these ideas were generated in the Eastern United States and in Western civilization as a whole. By and large, Western settlers appear to have been more imitative than original in their political institutions. The case for the West as a special source of individualism is similarly mixed. It is possible to point to a fairly strong stream of Western demands for governmental interference of one kind or another from the days of internal improvements to the age of railroad regulation, parity and price supports.

One of the most criticized aspects of Turner's conception of American history, the so-called safety-valve thesis, maintains that the availability of free land as a refuge for the oppressed and discontented has alleviated American social conflicts, minimized industrial strife, and contributed to the backwardness of the American labor movement. As Turner expressed it, the American worker was never compelled to accept inferior wages because he could "with a slight effort" reach free country and set up in farming. "Whenever social conditions tended to crystallize in the East, whenever capital tended to impede the freedom of the mass, there was this gate of escape to the free conditions of the frontier," where "free lands promoted individualism, economic equality, freedom to rise, democracy."

The expression "free land" is itself misleading. Land was relatively cheap in the United States during the nineteenth century, but the difference between free land and cheap land was crucial. Up to 1820 the basic price of land was $2.00 an acre, and for years afterward it was $1.25. Slight as it may seem, this represented a large sum to the Eastern worker, whose wage was generally about $1.00 a day. Economic historians have estimated that during the 1850's, $1,000 represented a fairly typical cost for setting up a farm on virgin prairie land, or buying an established one; and the cost of transporting a worker's family from, say, Massachusetts or New York

to Illinois or Iowa was a serious additional burden. Farming, moreover, is no enterprise for an amateur, nor one at which he has a good chance of success. The value of "free land" in alleviating distress has been challenged by several writers who have pointed out that periods of depression were the very periods when it was most difficult for the Eastern worker to move. Scattered instances of working-class migration to the West can be pointed to, but detailed studies of the origins of migrants have failed to substantiate the Turner thesis.

The Homestead Act of 1862, which was designed to give family-size farms (up to 160 acres) to bona fide settlers, does not seem to have changed the picture drastically. It suggests an era of great bounty, which turns out upon examination to be illusory. By 1890, after a generation of hectic national growth, only about 372,000 farms had been entered and kept under the Homestead Act. In the meatime, about 180,-000,000 acres had been given by state and federal governments to the railroad companies, who held some of it and disposed of much at a considerable markup. Much of the best land was also withheld for sale by the government—and it usually went at prices well above the minimum of $2.50 an acre. Out of every six or seven acres that the government had given up by 1900, only one had gone to homesteaders. Unfortunately, the showing of the homesteaders was poorer than this figure indicates, for not all of them were legitimate. The administration of the Homestead Act was so hopelessly bad that scores upon scores of speculators, using dummies to masquerade their entries, secured parcels of land often running into tens of thousands of acres, and these lands passed into the

hands of farmers only after the speculators had taken their cut. As Roy M.
Robbins remarks in his study of *Our
Landed Heritage,* the period was one in
which "the corporate and capitalistic
forces had gained complete ascendancy
over the settler as the pioneering agent."
By 1900, 35.3 per cent of the farms in
this nation of "free land" were operated
by tenants.

In spite of these criticisms, something
has been salvaged from the safety-valve
thesis. Although the West was not filled
up by workers moving in time of depression, the evidence indicates that it
was filled up by farmers moving in times
of prosperity. In this way the presence
of available land is generally conceded
to have played an important part in re-
lieving *rural* discontent—the dominant
form of discontent in nineteenth-century
America. And it presumably had a
roundabout effect on the urban situation. In Europe the city was the characteristic haven of the surplus farm
population. Insofar as the comparable
surplus population of the United States
took another choice, migration further
West, instead of swelling the ranks of
the urban working class, there may have
been an indirect operation of the safety
valve. Its magnitude and importance
are uncertain.

But the safety valve principle also
operated in reverse, and it is a signal
weakness of the Turner version that it
concentrates attention on much the less
significant of two population movements. The dominant tide of migration
from 1860 to 1900 was not from East
to West, but from the farm to the city.
In forty years the farm population
grew by about nine million, while the
non-farm population grew by almost
thirty-six million. It was the cities that
received not only the bulk of the immigration from abroad, but also the bulk
of the surplus farm population. This
flow of the farm surplus to the cities
may have been intermittent, broken and
partially reversed during depression periods, but its net size is undeniable.
Fred A. Shannon has estimated that "at
least twenty farmers moved to town for
each industrial laborer who moved to
the land, and ten sons of farmers went to
the city for each one who became the
owner of a new farm anywhere in the
nation." It is possible that the acuteness
of the agrarian unrest of the 1890's can
be traced in some part to the fact that
the pace of city growth had slackened
off, and that this safety valve for the
farmers was beginning to fail. At any
rate, to follow the Turnerian emphasis
upon "free land" as a primary outlet,
and to ignore the migration to the cities,
is to perpetuate a major distortion of
American history.

Finally, Turner acknowledged but
failed to see the full importance for his
thesis of the fact that the United States
not only had a frontier but was a frontier—a major outlet for the countries of
Western Europe during the nineteenth
century. From 1820 to 1929, the total
European emigration to the United
States was more than 37,500,000—a number only a million short of the entire
population of the United States in 1870.
In one decade alone, 1901-1910, 8,795,000
people came from Europe. If Europe
shared to such a major extent in this
safety-valve economy, its uniqueness for
American development must be considerably modified. The mingling of peoples that took place in the United States
must be placed alongside the presence
of "free land" in explaining American
development; the closure of the Ameri-

can gates after the First World War becomes an historical event of broader significance than the disappearance of the frontier line in 1890. And the facts of immigration probably provide a better key to the character of the American labor movement than any speculation about the effects of "free hand" upon workers who could not reach it.

It should be added, in justice to Turner, that his historical writing was better than his frontier thesis, and not least because he regularly made use in practice of historical factors which were not accounted for in his theory. Although he often stated his ideas with the vigor of a propagandist, his was not a doctrinaire mind, and he was willing, as time went on, to add new concepts to his analysis. In 1925 he went so far as to admit the need of "an urban reinterpretation of our history." "I hope," he frequently said, "to propagate inquiry, not to produce disciples." In fact he did both, but he propagated less inquiry among his disciples than among his critics.

Just as the reaction of the 1930s and 1940s against the frontier thesis attracted support from scholars in many disciplines, so the revival of interest in the hypothesis of the 1950s and 1960s has converted students of different backgrounds into defenders of Frederick Jackson Turner. Of these, none has argued more plausibly than HARRY C. ALLEN (1917–), Commonwealth Fund Professor at the University College, London. Educated at Oxford and with experience in the academic communities of several countries including Australia and the United States, Allen brings to the study of the frontier thesis a perspective broadened by his international background. Although further evidence supporting his viewpoint has been advanced since he wrote this essay in 1957, it remains one of the most persuasive statements of the Turnerian position.*

► *The Thesis Upheld*

Reaction from his influence was no doubt inevitable, and it has certainly not lacked in vigour. For the past twenty-five years he has been assailed from all sides by an increasing army of critics, two of the more vehement of whom (Louis M. Hacker and James C. Malin) have not hesitated to describe the Turner tradition, the one as "not only fictitious but also to a very large extent positively harmful", and the other as having "unsound and vicious methodology and philosophy". This was not merely the customary revolt of one generation against its predecessor, but was also a product of the development of in-creasingly specialized historical research; Turner was one of the great historical generalizers, and none of them has escaped altogether from the assaults of the specialists. In the same way, for instance, did the once venerable Whig interpretation of English history fall into disrepute. This constant process of contemporary correction of historical error is entirely proper, but it should not be conducted with such violence or venom that the right conclusions disappear along with the wrong ones and that future historians are frightened to try and replace bad generalizations by good. There are firm grounds for thinking that the reaction

* H. C. Allen, "F. J. Turner and the Frontier in American History," H. C. Allen and C. P. Hill, eds., *British Essays in American History* (London, Edward Arnold (Publishers) Ltd., 1957), pp. 150–166. Reprinted by permission of the publisher and H. C. Allen.

against Turner has gone too far, and that his critics have in their turn laid themselves open to criticism. Indeed there are already signs of a counter-attack; as Robert E. Reigel suggests, "The time seems to have arrived when the bickering over Turner . . . should be replaced by the formulation of a new set of generalizations based upon the researches of the past half century."

This process is already under way, and one aspect of it should be a rehabilitation of Turner himself. In a number of cases a general reconsideration of Turner's view and that of his critics on a particular issue leaves a remarkable proportion of his thesis standing—far more indeed sometimes than of the critical antithesis. "Simplest of the accusations against Turner", for example, in Riegel's words, "was that he had used his terms so vaguely and with so many different meanings that precision was impossible." As the most specific of his critics on this score, George Wilson Pierson, complained, "the frontier was not merely *place* and *population,* that is to say a savage wilderness and a sparse society of trappers, herders and pioneers. It was also *process,* or more specifically the processes of conquering the continent, of moving westward, of changing from Europeans into Americans. Whether such irregularity in definition can any longer be tolerated is a question" for very serious consideration. But does such criticism really invalidate Turner's thesis? The use of a single term with many meanings is not necessarily a loose usage, and if it corresponds with reality, the more compendious the meaning and the more succinct the word the better. There does not seem to be anything wrong or really confusing about associating the place, the people and the process

with the single name "frontier"; indeed, the very reverse appears to be the case, for it was Turner's real achievement to make this single word the key to so much in American history. An analogous term much used by medieval historians seems to be very similar and also very satisfactory—"the marches". It conjures up, without difficulty and with illuminating effect, an image not only of a kind of place, but also of the kind of people who were important in that place, and even of the process by which they developed a new and special kind of social structure. In fact, the concept of the American frontier can sometimes be more easily understood by the English student in terms of the medieval march than in terms of any more modern parallel. Yet this semantic criticism of Turner has been widely accepted in practice as undermining his whole thesis, a sweeping result which does not seem to be entirely justified by a reconsideration of the evidence: on the contrary, it seems to leave Turner's original use of the term remarkably unscathed.

Indeed what seems in some ways most remarkable about his ideas, sixty years after they were first put forward and thirty years after his death, is how extraordinarily right they are in their major contentions. By no means all the criticisms were, of course, too severe and not many of them can be disregarded altogether: most of Turner's ideas have needed filling-out and a number have needed correction. But when all is said and done, they contained a very small proportion of dross. This is true even of such a very general question as the whole context in which he saw the importance of the American frontier. Perhaps the important disservice done to Turner by his followers was to exaggerate his emphasis on the uniqueness of the American frontier experience by studying it almost entirely in isolation. (It was no coincidence that in political, as well as historical, affairs, Turner's followers were of a generation that was far more isolationist than Turner.) This subtle twist which was given to the background of the frontier as Turner saw it was also characteristic of the process by which words were put into his mouth by others. There is no doubt that in his mind the development of the American frontier remained an integral part of European and Western history, although it is not so immediately apparent in his writings that he felt it to be so.

This was the case even though he was primarily concerned to demonstrate that the importance of the European origins of American society had been grossly over-emphasized in the past. It came out very clearly in his teaching, one of the great virtues of which was that he brought his students to a fascinated realization, as Craven wrote, that "local history was human history". Turner's mind had been stimulated by, and was well furnished with, a wide knowledge of the development of the ancient and modern world. In his early years he even taught courses on ancient and general European history as well as on European history in the nineteenth century, and it was not uncharacteristic that he wrote in 1891: "Even here in young America old Rome still lives . . . not only is it true that no country can be understood without taking account of all the past; it is also true that we cannot select a stretch of land and say we will limit our study to this land; for local history can only be understood in the light of the history of the world." This broad sense of perspective was lost in the parochialism and

indeed chauvinism of some of the agents of the reaction against the "germ theory" of political history which Turner began.

We are now in a position to restore that sense of perspective and to see the American experience as part of the experience of mankind. The frontier of the United States was one among many; it was but a part, as W. P. Webb has pointed out, of "the great frontier" of Western civilization. The expansion of the United States was merely one aspect of the huge expansion of the European peoples into the sparsely settled areas of the globe, which took place between the fifteenth and the twentieth centuries. American beef, Southern cotton, and Northern wheat were the counterparts of Australian wool and New Zealand mutton. In many respects, however, the American was the most remarkable of the frontiers, and it was the good fortune of the American people that their land was both potentially rich and actually thinly populated and that their lines of communication with Western Europe were relatively short and direct. The great Atlantic waterway nurtured the growth of the United States in an economic sense long after political separation had taken place, and the link between British capital and manufactures exported to the United States and the westward movement of the American people was much closer and lasted far longer than American historians have sometimes recognized. Without the Industrial Revolution, which had its origin and for a long time its centre in Britain, the expansion of the American frontier could never have proceeded at the speed which it in fact attained. Although of unique significance it has nevertheless been an integral part of Atlantic history, which by the date of its closing was fast becoming (although the fact has not even now been recognized by many historians) the only fully significant form of Western history. Such a development was not as alien to the thought of Turner as to that of some of his followers.

Thus it is that in other respects also Turner's views stand up much better to the criticism to which they have been subjected than has often been admitted. It is not possible here to analyze his views in detail, but it may be useful tentatively to suggest a few conclusions about the frontier which can be maintained today even in the face of Turner's critics; and it will be found that in outline these conclusions still follow with notable fidelity the contours of his original work. This was, of course, that of a pioneer, and his map lacks much of the detail which has been found necessary by later cartographers; it was a sketch-map which needed checking and augmenting. A great deal of this has been done, but little overall reconsideration of his thesis has been attempted. The complexity of frontier history, the variegated forms which the opening up of the West took, has made and still makes generalization hazardous. Yet a certain majestic uniformity does characterize the westward movement as such, albeit in the early years of the republic the drives north into upper New England, and, even more particularly, south into lower Georgia and Florida were also of great importance. But although the main flow of the current was unmistakable and apparently irreversible, when observed more closely even the periods of swiftest impetus to the West can be seen to have incorporated many diverse types of frontier and of frontier activity: each wave upon the shore was at once similar in outline to its successor yet vastly different

in detailed structure. Of these many different forms of frontier, some tended to recur frequently, and sometimes to do so in similar sequence, though this repetitive pattern was, as is the way of human history, never uniform or exact....

He was right also when he pointed out the importance of "free land" in American development. It may be that Turner paid too little attention to the land speculator and that he sometimes seemed to imply that the exploitation of the unsettled lands of the West by an overflowing population from the East was more direct than at times it actually was, but the availability of vast and virtually unoccupied lands on the frontier must obviously have been one of the most important conditioning factors in America's growth, as a glance at the contrasting situation in the older and more settled countries of western Europe shows. Turner was very aware of the economic and political importance of the issue of cheap land in the first century of American independence, and subsequent research has in fact shown clearly that the years 1800-1862 in American land legislation saw an increasingly successful series of efforts to replace the Hamiltonian idea of land as a source of Federal revenue by the Jeffersonian belief in cheap land as the birthright of a democratic people, which took legislative shape in progressive provisions for the acquiring of smaller and smaller minimum lots of public land at lower and lower prices. That this movement had at heart the interests of the small pioneer farmer is indicated by the tendency of both large Southern planters and great eastern employers of labour to oppose it, and by the fact that the Homestead Act of 1862 allowed virtually any adult to apply for a quarter-section, or 160 acres, of public land for a fee of $10, designed to cover only administrative costs. Even though conditions were to change radically as the frontier entered the arid West, and thus to render the Homestead Act itself much less important than had been hoped, or than has sometimes been supposed since, the type of frontiersman whom Turner had in mind was able to dominate the land legislation of the nation in the most critical years of its development. This historical figure, the small pioneer farmer, is, if not quite so unchallenged in importance as Turner's followers supposed, a much more real one, and a much surer foundation for generalization concerning the American frontier, than his critics have allowed.

These generalizations are many, and they are so important because the frontier deeply affected the lives and habits and also the personalities of those who lived upon it, and through them of their children and their children's children, for, as Turner pointed out, the frontier influence passed insensibly from father to son, until it became part of the American heritage. There is no corner of the United States that has not been on the frontier at some time in the last three hundred and fifty years, and perhaps a half of its territory has been subdued within the last century. Although only a relatively small part of America has been frontier at any particular moment (indeed, as G. W. Pierson has pointed out, the proportion of the American people who actually lived on the frontier decreased steadily throughout American history), until about 1890 the frontier tradition profoundly modified the way of life even of those Americans who spent their lives far away from it in great cities.

Since that time other factors, such as American industrial might and the increasing pressure of foreign affairs, have altered the inherited pattern of American life, but even in the case of nations the character and ideas acquired in youth are very difficult to alter, at all events with any speed, so that the significance of the frontier in American history must still be reckoned almost as considerable as Turner believed.

Nor need we reject his views as to the way in which the frontier affected America quite as absolutely as some of his critics would have us. Modifications of his thesis are certainly necessary, but it still contains a solid stratum of truth. One of his primary contentions, for example, was that the frontier was the line of most rapid and effective Americanization. In the colonial period this seems very likely to have been true, because few parts of the colonies were in fact far away from the frontier and its influence, as the western experiences of a Tidewater Virginian like Washington may serve to illustrate. After independence the frontier began to move more swiftly and to leave ever more extensive settled areas behind it, but it had already made an indelible imprint upon the American character. The predominantly North-European immigrants of the first half of the nineteenth century seem to have found their way in considerable numbers to the developing rural areas of the Middle West; the South absorbed relatively few of the newcomers, because of the existence of Negro slavery, although the frontier even of the lower Mississippi valley certainly remained a line of effective Americanization in the days of Andrew Jackson. But, setting aside the Irish who tended often to gather in the urban areas, the characteristic new American, even as late as 1860, probably settled in regions where the pioneer farmer or his immediate successor was the dominating figure, as in Wisconsin in the days of Turner's youth. After the Civil War the huge waves of "new immigrants" went overwhelmingly to the great cities, and it was here that the process of assimilation had increasingly to take place, but it was a good deal slower and less effective than it had been, while rural America still provided, under the influence of Jefferson, the ideal pattern for American society, certainly down to the Populist era and perhaps even to that of Wilson. The Jeffersonian idolum was not effectively replaced by one more suited to the realities of life in a great industrial community until the days of the New Deal. Thus it can be maintained that the frontier was *a* line of rapid and effective Americanization throughout its existence, and *the* line of most rapid and effective Americanization during the formative years of American history.

In the same way Turner held that the frontier had a nationalizing tendency, that it strengthened the hands of the federal as opposed to the state governments, because almost all the states except the original thirteen grew up under the aegis of the Union and therefore their citizens had more feeling for the nation as a whole than for their particular states. This opinion has been little criticized and seems valid still. Equally uncontested in his view that the frontier helped to make Americans prodigal, indeed wasteful, in their use of the seemingly inexhaustible natural resources of their country. Here, despite the rise during his lifetime of a conservation movement of which he strongly approved, the mark upon American life,

both in city and country, is still plain to see: never perhaps has there been a whole society so uninhibited and so ruthless in the exploitation of the bounty of its natural environment. Yet another of Turner's theses has not been very seriously disputed, that which pointed out that the harsh and pressing realities of frontier life left little time for the refinements of civilization, so that there was a certain crudeness in the American way of life. That a reaction against this set in, in favour of the cultivation which prosperity made possible, was natural and does not invalidate the main argument, which receives ample support not only from the offensive comments of many British visitors to the West in the nineteenth century, but also from the long cultural dominance of the East.

Much more contentious has been his assertion that the most important effect of the frontier has been the promotion of democracy in the United States and in Europe. Critics have pointed out that not many democratic processes were invented in frontier areas, and that many reforms had their origin in the East. This is true, but less harmful to Turner's contention than has been maintained. The history of older societies in Europe clearly shows that it was not so much the invention as the adoption of democratic ideas that was difficult: the seeds of most new ideas have long existed in some form or other, and their need is always a fruitful soil and a favourable climate in which to germinate. This the frontier provided. There was some democratic thought in England in the seventeenth century, and much by the early nineteenth, but many years were to pass before it was generally accepted or actually put into practice. The fundamental reason for this was the power of vested interests, and even more of fixed habits and prejudices, and Turner rightly claimed that the effect of the frontier was to destroy many of these, and to reduce man, as an economic and political animal, to his simplest basic elements. The result was a national atmosphere in which increasingly one man tended to regard himself as the equal of the next and in which the ideas of democracy naturally flourished; thus it has yet to be demonstrated that any narrow oligarchical constitutions existed in the Middle West (even in the south of which democracy was for the white man a powerful reality) whereas it has been clearly shown that plenty of the new states in the area had democratic governing processes from their first entry into the Union. Even more striking is the fact that a number of western states held second constitutional conventions within two decades of their admission to the Union, and that the new constitutions produced by them tended to be more democratic than the original ones, partly no doubt because they embodied the western experience of the settlers. Indeed it is still hard to see how it can be disputed that the adoption of democratic ideas proceeded very swiftly in the West and that the great popular movements found much of their support in areas where frontier conditions had recently prevailed. Few Europeans, for instance, who have visited the excellent reconstruction of the village at New Salem from which Lincoln sought election to the legislature of Illinois as the representative of Sangamon County in 1832, can have any serious doubt of the reality of frontier democracy or the depth of its influence. From it grew Lincoln's profound conviction that the future of popular government in the world depended peculiarly upon the United States, and in this sense it is still possible to maintain that one of the most significant effects of the frontier has been the promotion of democracy.

Among the most influential of Turner's dicta was that which declared that the frontier encouraged self-reliance and individualism. Of the pioneer farmer, the dominating frontier figure of the years before the Civil War, this was intensely true; this independent practical landowner was the classic Jeffersonian and Jacksonian democrat. Turner and his followers may have over-emphasized these qualities; some critics have pointed out, for instance, that in many ways the life of the frontier essentially depended upon mutual assistance. But this has never really been denied; it has seldom been asserted that many men (let alone women) actively enjoyed the hardships of frontier existence, but the fact remains that they endured them, and if they survived no doubt took a good deal of pride in the fact that they did so. Nor is it reasonable to compare the occasional, although essentially necessary, co-operation of individuals on the frontier —in the log-rolling and other assistance, for instance, without which a log-cabin could not be built—with the insensible everyday dependence of the individual upon society which is characteristic of more settled areas; to do so implies a certain lack of sense of proportion, for to emphasize the self-reliance of frontiersmen is not to assert that they were self-sufficient. Nor must too much be made of the criticism of the reality of frontier individualism which points out that the individuals were in fact remarkably alike, that all along the frontier these individualists were asserting their independence of each other in precisely similar ways. Individualism need not necessarily be eccentricity, and if individuals, even in isolation, did not react in similar ways to similar stimuli, any form of society, and in particular any democratic system of government, would be quite impracticable. Fine distinctions between shades of red must not blind historians who make them to the more important difference between red and blue; if we compare it for a moment to a closed society like that of many countries in Europe, we can still agree that, at least up to the Civil War, the American frontier was a breeding ground for self-reliance and individualism.

After this date a change did take place. The pioneer toughness, the readiness to resort to direct and even violent methods to attain political and economic ends, which was characteristic of all frontier life in America—and indeed to some extent elsewhere—remained; but nature decreed that the ratio of individual to social effort should alter radically, so that the individual found himself able to achieve far less than he had been able to heretofore without calling society to his aid. As Webb has pointed out, men were forced when they launched forth upon the Great Plains to adjust the habits which they had acquired in a forested area to suit the treeless prairie, and as they entered the zone between approximately the 96th and the 100th meridians they began to feel the full effect of an even more formidable change, that of increasing aridity. For a period it was concealed by a cycle of years of better-than-average rainfall and by the highly fluctuating nature of that rainfall, but, at the cost of great hardship and suffering in such states as Kansas, the lesson was in due course learned that the small pioneer farmer could no longer

function as he had been able to do farther east, and that even the large-scale farmer needed more and more help from society the farther he moved into the arid and later mountainous regions of the West. Men could only prosper on the land by enlarging their holdings and relying increasingly upon pastoral husbandry, or by calling upon society for aid in the form of improved agricultural techniques or of irrigation. Thus, whereas in the fertile lands over which the frontier had previously passed a man could make a very satisfactory living off 160 or even 80 acres, in the West it was pretty nearly impossible on 320, let alone 160. Unless his land was irrigated, a farmer on the Great Plains needed between 360 and 640 acres and a rancher there or farther west anything between 2000 and 50,000 acres. This inexorable fact was reflected in the general tenor of land legislation after the Civil War, by which the long Jeffersonian trend toward smaller holdings was surely, if covertly, reversed. Between 1873 and 1889 a number of measures were passed by Congress which made greater maximum holdings possible without greatly increasing their price. At the same time there developed an increasing reliance on the co-operation of farmers one with another, as in co-operatives, and on the new scientific methods developed by the technicians of society at large, such as those for dry farming.

Although it only began to develop on a large scale after the frontier was officially closed, it is the history of irrigation which most clearly illustrates this increased reliance of the individual pioneer upon society, as soon as he enters an arid zone, for it is only possible where there is centralized control over the actions of many persons. Normally this can only be exercised by one authority, the state, and in mid-nineteenth-century America, even more than mid-nineteenth-century Britain, there was very general aversion from state interference in economic affairs. It is thus most interesting that the great pioneers of irrigation were the Mormons. This was not only because they moved much farther into the semi-desert lands much earlier than any other settlers, but also because their Church of Jesus Christ of the Latter-day Saints exercised a very close supervision over the whole life of the community, so that Brigham Young in his wisdom was able to invest ownership and distribution of the vital waters running down from the mountains of the Wasatch Range in the church. This produced a uniquely successful system of irrigation many years before the pressure of circumstances had forced Americans to accept large-scale state action to alleviate, among other things, the difficulties arising from the aridity of the West. This acceptance by the state of a positive economic role in the life of the people owed much to the harsh conditions of life in arid frontier regions; it was promoted, too, by the growth of industrialism and the rise of socialism and trade unionism which began in Europe, but it also had grass roots, for the fundamental basis of Populism was agrarian. The Granger movement, which started as a non-political alliance of farmers for economic ends, before long fostered in the hearts of its members a determination to assert their political power to attain those ends. By capturing a numer of state governments, the outraged farmers were able to enforce government control over some of the economic practices which they disliked, as for example by the regulation of abuses arising from the existence of great railroad monopolies. The difficulties of the frontier in the West in the last quarter of the nineteenth century forced men to rely less on themselves and more upon one another and upon the state.

Critics of Turner have objected vigorously to his elastic use of the term frontier to cover the settled areas of the West, such as, for example, Kansas in 1890; this identification of the frontier with the West seems to them unjustified. But this objection not only shortens the perspective of history, it ignores Turner's point that the United States is like a palimpsest, with the influence of the frontier embedded at each level. The frontier, for instance, was not far below the surface in Nebraska in 1896; in 1860 its population had been 20,000, and by 1890 was over a million, yet many a young man of the former year was still in the prime of political activity in the campaign of 1896. To ascribe to such areas the character of frontier societies seems far from unreasonable, and it is not wildly absurd to do so even to certain areas of the South which played a part in the Populist movement.

Of this lessening of the degree of self-reliance and individualism which was possible on the frontier, Turner was well aware; he saw that the small pioneer farmer could no longer succeed unaided in the arid West, and that, with the channelling of frontier energies into political agitation, the state would have to play a much greater part in the economic development of the country. He was too close to the event to appreciate, as can now be done, how greatly the peculiar conditions of aridity in the West, by encouraging economic reliance on the state, prepared the way for the new position of government in the American industrial society of the twentieth century. The ease of transition from the overwhelmingly rural Democracy of Jackson and the predominantly rural Democracy of Bryan to the largely urban Democracy of Woodrow Wilson and Franklin D. Roosevelt owed much to this historical chance, for although it is possible to exaggerate the reluctance of state, and even federal, authorities to play an active economic role in the first century after independence (as the whole history of the demand for internal improvements shows), the transformation of a *laisser-faire* rural nation into an industrial society with an increasing element of government control would have been much harder without the particular preparation afforded by the Populism of the West.

Turner was greatly concerned to point out that the closing of the frontier could be expected to have—as it has had—profound effects upon the development of American life, and it is on one notion arising from his ideas on this subject that he has been most powerfully attacked, the safety-valve theory; but it should be remembered that he himself never fully or explicitly formulated this concept which was greatly—and sometimes rashly—elaborated by his disciples, and which had in any event existed in an inchoate form even before his time. It is now clear that after 1860 only relatively minute numbers of settlers went from the industrial areas direct to the frontier in the capacity of farmers, though the situation before that date is by no means so clear, and in all periods the extent to which non-farmers were able to move west as the basic development of agriculture made possible more complex economic growth (acting in fact as a kind of economic multiplier) needs

careful investigation. But whatever the reservations one must make, for many thousands of families the frontier in America offered better possibilities for a good and growing livelihood on their own land than anywhere else in the world, a fact which sank deep into the American consciousness, so that even after 1860 most of his fellow-countrymen believed with Turner that free land meant free opportunities. The myth, if such it be, associated with the words, "Go west, young man", was possibly almost as successful in allaying discontent as the reality would have been, for what men believe is usually the decisive factor in their actions; many Americans no doubt more patiently bore those evils that they had because they believed that a way of escape always existed for them, although they could never actually bring themselves to take it. In any case, as Riegel writes, "While a good case can be made that the frontier had no real effect on eastern population concentration, such a conclusion seems to affront common sense . . . The occupation and exploitation of an entire continent with no effect on population concentration seems incredible."

In the same way Turner has been attacked by some historians, particularly those influenced by Marxist ideas, because his thesis largely ignored the importance of class in the development of American society. Most of this criticism came in the thirties when the Great Depression had undermined faith in the traditional "American" virtues, and it was very unhistorical, for when Turner published his most influential essay in 1893 it was, despite the growing inequalities of wealth which sprang from the new industrialism, emphatically still true that the remarkable thing about America had until quite recently been the political and social democracy which the abundance of land had chiefly made possible. Even to the present day the habits of mind acquired in those early years have done much to prevent that stiffening of the nation's social and economic joints which is often the bane of older societies. In modern America social equality is a potent ideal and class distinctions are less important than in the life of most other peoples. For this fact the frontier was in part responsible. If Turner is to blame here it is because he did not sufficiently modify his own views in later life when circumstances had changed, but there was in any case no call for him to do so except of the most recent years, for before then he was on solid ground.

Broad generalizations about whole societies are always difficult and seldom absolutely true, but it is not really possible to doubt the deep and lasting influence of the frontier upon the history of the United States, nor to question that it directly contributed to the formation of many of the most pronounced characteristics of the American people. It cannot be doubted, to give another instance, that it encouraged their optimism and their idealism, as Turner claimed. Because that optimism was usually justified it does not mean that there have not always been more gloomy traits in the American character: it simply means that cheerfulness was normally uppermost, if only because the pessimistic and the weak had often gone to the wall already. Idealism, too, was a vital force in their lives, even if their primary objectives were, as critics have pointed out, largely economic; few men are not deeply, often fundamentally, motivated by material needs, and what was im-

portant about the Americans was that they were also moved by political and social ideals of a high order. Both idealism and optimism were in the end encouraged by the frontier, despite the pessimism of such observers as *Martin Chuzzlewit* and the "realistic" novelists of the Great Plains; indeed, as the story of Per Hansa in *Giants in the Earth* so clearly shows, conjoined in the form of hope (which never had greater call to spring eternal in the human breast) optimism and idealism *had* to be part of the equipment of those who successfully braved the terrible rigours of the frontier.

> And the west wind blew in the faces
>   of Dickon's sons
> And they looked to the West and
>   searched it with their eyes,
> And there was the endless forest and
>   the sharp star.

But they needed more than that to conquer and subdue a continental domain of three million square miles. They needed great ingenuity and prodigious energy, and Turner was right to call attention to the existence of both among the frontiersmen. Concerning his claim that they displayed ingenuity in adapting themselves to changed conditions of life on the frontiers of civilization, critics have declared that in fact they only adapted themselves slowly to changes in physical environment, and cite their delay in leaving the forests to tackle the Great Plains as an instance. Yet the whole process, not merely of adaptation but of complete occupation, took barely half a century. Half a century! Let them see the Frenchman still ploughing with his ox! None but an American could have thought of such a comment, a fact which is in itself a tribute to the depth of the frontier influence. If the criticism is taken further and it is claimed that very few inventions were actually made on the frontier, let it be remembered that, in economic as in political affairs, it is not the devising of new techniques, but the speed of their adoption—whatever their origin—which is the fundamental condition of great and rapid development. The frontier encouraged the existing Yankee virtues of ingenuity and resourcefulness.

Above all, however, it fostered that driving, furious energy which is perhaps the most striking and characteristic of all the features of American life. It not only pervades the history of every phase of the American frontier, but also permeates city as well as country throughout the land; even the South, with its "lazy, crooning, comforting tongue", swallowed up the vast Black Belt of cotton lands in little more than fifty years. The "rolling, restless wave of seeking men", surging "westward and westward, killing down the day", is at the very heart of the American experience, and the indomitable expansion of the people of the United States across their continental domain has fired the imagination not only of the Americans but also of many foreign observers and historians. It is impossible not to believe with Turner that this consummate achievement has been of profound and enduring significance for America, and, through her, for mankind.

Guide for Further Reading

Frederick Jackson Turner's essays have been collected in three volumes: *The Early Writings of Frederick Jackson Turner* (Madison, 1938), *The Frontier in American History* (New York, 1920), and *The Significance of Sections in American History* (New York, 1932). He also published two books that shed occasional light on his theory: *Rise of the New West, 1819–1829* (New York, 1906), and *The United States, 1830–1850: the Nation and Its Sections* (New York, 1935). The essays dealing with frontier theory have been gathered in Ray A. Billington, Ed., *Frontier and Section: Selected Essays of Frederick Jackson Turner* (Englewood Cliffs, N. J., 1961). Unpublished essays found in Turner's papers have been published as Wilbur R. Jacobs, Ed., *Frederick Jackson Turner's Legacy* (San Marino, Calif., 1965).

That the frontier had influenced the American character was recognized long before Turner formulated his thesis in 1893. This subject is briefly reviewed in Herman C. Nixon, "Precursors of Turner in the Interpretation of the American Frontier," *South Atlantic Quarterly*, vol. 28 (January 1929), pp. 83–98. Lee Benson, "The Historical Background of Turner's Frontier Essay," *Agricultural History*, vol. 25 (April 1951), pp. 59–82, reveals the degree to which Turner was influenced by the intellectual atmosphere of his day. The same author insists that Turner borrowed his ideas from an Italian writer in "Achille Loria's Influence on American Economic Thought: Including His Contributions to the Frontier Hypothesis," *Agri-*cultural History, vol. 24 (October 1950), pp. 182–199. A searching examination of the origin of Turner's historical ideas is in Fulmer Mood, "The Development of Frederick Jackson Turner as a Historical Thinker," Colonial Society of Massachusetts, *Transactions, 1937–1942*, vol. 34 (1943), pp. 283–352.

Several historians have interested themselves in Turner and his historical methodology. No biography exists, but an excellent brief sketch of his life is in Merle Curti, *Frederick Jackson Turner* (Mexico, D. F., 1949), reprinted in O. Lawrence Burnette, Jr., Comp., *Wisconsin Witness to Frederick Jackson Turner* (Madison, Wis., 1961). Turner's historical methods are examined in the same author's "The Section and the Frontier in American History: The Methodological Concepts of Frederick Jackson Turner," in Stuart A. Rice, Ed., *Methods in Social Science. A Case Book* (Chicago, 1931), pp. 353–367. Another sympathetic evaluation of his role as historian is in Carl Becker, "Frederick Jackson Turner," in Howard W. Odum, Ed., *American Masters of Social Science* (New York, 1927), pp. 273–318. Two articles by Avery Craven also shed light on the man and his ideas: "Frederick Jackson Turner," in William T. Hutchinson, Ed., *Marcus W. Jernegan Essays in American Historiography* (Chicago, 1937), pp. 252–270, and "Frederick Jackson Turner, Historian," *Wisconsin Magazine of History*, vol. 25 (June, 1942, pp. 408–424. A modern appraisal, based on the Frederick Jackson Turner

119

papers in the Henry E. Huntington Library and Art Gallery, is Wilbur R. Jacobs, "Frederick Jackson Turner," *The American West*, vol. 1 (Winter 1964), pp. 32–35, 78–79.

The extensive literature of the 1930s and 1940s attacking the frontier thesis is listed and appraised in Gene M. Gressley, "The Turner Thesis—A Problem in Historiography," *Agricultural History*, vol. 32 (October 1958), 227–249, and Walter Rundell, Jr., "Concepts of the 'Frontier' and the 'West'," *Arizona and the West*, vol. 1 (Spring 1959), pp. 13–41. A somewhat fuller discussion, which includes more recent appraisals of Turner's work, is Ray A. Billington, *The American Frontier* (2d ed., Washington, 1965).

The assault on the thesis began with the publication of John C. Almack, "The Shibboleth of the Frontier," *Historical Outlook*, vol. 16 (May 1925), pp. 197–202, which argued generally that the frontier had hindered rather than stimulated cultural progress. It was continued by Louis M. Hacker, who in "Sections or Classes?" *The Nation*, vol. 137 (July 26, 1933) and other essays condemned Turner for ignoring the class struggle and other economic forces. George W. Pierson entered the conflict with the essay reproduced in this volume; he continued the attack with "The Frontier and American Institutions. A Criticism of the Turner Theory," *New England Quarterly*, vol. 15 (June 1942), pp. 224–255; both essays condemned Turner for the manner in which his theory had been expressed as well as for the theory itself. A similar general assault was written by Murray Kane, "Some Considerations on the Frontier Concept of Frederick Jackson Turner," *Mississippi Valley Historical Review*, vol. 27 (December 1940), pp. 379–400.

Other critics of the frontier thesis focused on particular issues or charged that the hypothesis has exerted a harmful effect on the people of the United States. James C. Malin, "Space and History: Reflections on the Closed-Space Doctrines of Turner and Mackinder," *Agricultural History*, vol. 18 (April 1944), pp. 65–74, and (July 1944), pp. 107–126, held that Turner's stress on a geographic frontier had blinded Americans to other frontiers in science and technology, and made them receptive to governmental infringements on their liberties. Carlton J. H. Hayes, in "The American Frontier—Frontier of What?" *American Historical Review*, vol. 51 (January 1946), pp. 199–216, insisted that the hypothesis had intensified American nationalism at a time when internationalism was to the world's benefit. Many of these arguments were summarized in the general article by Richard Hofstadter, which is republished here.

More specific critics believed that the frontier thesis was too narrowly oriented and that important phases of life were ignored. W. Eugene Shiels, "The Frontier Hypothesis: A Corollary," *Mid-America*, vol. 17 (January 1935), pp. 3–9, charged Turner with ignoring religious factors. More searching was the volume by Henry Nash Smith, *Virgin Land: The American West as Symbol and Myth* (Cambridge, Mass., 1950), built on the thesis that two frontiers had actually existed, one real and the other imaginary, and that the myth of the frontier had influenced Turner's description of the real frontier. Many of the extensive writings on comparative frontiers were also critical of the Turnerians; these have been summarized in an article by Marvin Mikesell, "Comparative Studies in Frontier History," *Annals of the Association of American Geographers*, vol. 50 (March 1960), pp. 62–74, and in Dietrich Gerhard, "The Frontier in Comparative View," *Comparative Studies in Society and History*, vol. 1 (March 1959), pp. 205–229.

The controversy among scholars over the validity of the safety-valve doctrine began with the publication of Carter Goodrich and Sol Davison, "The Wage-Earner in the Westward Movement," *Political Science Quarterly*, vol. 50 (June 1935), pp. 161–185, and vol. 51 (March 1936), pp. 61–116, and Murray Kane, "Some Considerations on the Safety Valve Doctrine," *Mississippi Valley Historical Review*, vol. 23 (September 1936), pp. 169–188. Both articles used statistics to demonstrate that migration declined in depression periods, and that few actual wage earners moved west. They were answered by one of Turner's most devoted disciples, Joseph Schafer, in several articles, the most important being "Concerning the Frontier as Safety Valve," *Political Science Quarterly,* vol. 52 (September 1937), pp. 407–420, and "Was the West a Safety Valve for Labor?" *Mississippi Valley Historical Review,* vol. 24 (December 1937), pp. 299-314. During the next few years two other authors rose to the attack: Rufus S. Tucker, "The Frontier as an Outlet for Surplus Labor," *Southern Economic Journal,* vol. 7 (October 1940), pp. 158–186 showed that after 1840 urban areas gained population more rapidly than rural, while Clarence H. Danhof, "Farm-Making Costs and the 'Safety Valve': 1850–1860," *Journal of Political Economy,* vol. 49 (June 1941), pp. 317–359, argued that farm-making costs were too high to allow wage earners to move to the frontier. Fred A. Shannon, whose article is in this book, climaxed the attack by attempting to demonstrate that even an indirect safety valve did not operate after 1860.

The recent reevaluation of the doctrine began with the publication of Norman J. Simler, "The Safety-Valve Doctrine Re-Evaluated," *Agricultural History,* vol. 32 (October 1958), pp. 250–257, and was continued in George G. S. Murphy and Arnold Zellner, "Sequential Growth, the Labor-Safety-Valve Doctrine and the Development of American Unionism," *Journal of Political Economy,* vol. 19 (September 1959), pp. 402–421. Both articles insisted on the validity of the doctrine, basing their conclusions on an examination of the total economy. The additional evidence supplied by Ellen von Nardroff in the article printed in this volume was questioned by Henry M. Littlefield largely on semantic grounds, "Has the Safety Valve Come Back to Life?" *Agricultural History,* vol. 28 (January 1964), pp. 47–49.

The Turnerian belief that democracy originated on the frontier was first challenged in two articles by Benjamin F. Wright, Jr.; one is published in this volume and the other was entitled "Political Institutions and the Frontier," in Dixon R. Fox, Ed., *Sources of Culture in the Middle West* (New York, 1934), pp. 15–38. Both maintain that democratic theory and practice developed in Europe and moved westward. Thomas P. Abernethy, "Democracy and the Southern Frontier," *Journal of Southern History,* vol. 4 (February 1938), pp. 3–13, holds that pioneer life in the South did not stimulate democracy. The first serious attack on this viewpoint was in Stanley Elkins and Eric McKitrick, "A Meaning for Turner's Frontier," *Political Science Quarterly,* vol. 69 (July 1954), pp. 321–353 and (December 1954), pp. 562–602; basing their study on local institutions, they showed that democracy did progress more rapidly on the frontier than in older communities. The books by Merle Curti and John D. Barnhart reprinted in part in this volume carried this analysis a step further. Roy F. Nichols, "The Territories: Seedbeds of Democracy," *Nebraska History,* vol. 35 (September 1954), pp. 159–172, shows that the repeated opportunity for constitution-making on successive frontiers stimulated experimentation that encouraged democracy.

Other writers have attacked or defended lesser aspects of the frontier thesis. That pioneer life stimulated individualism was questioned in Mody C. Boatright, "The Myth of Frontier Individualism," *Southwestern Social Science Quarterly,* vol. 22 (June 1941), pp. 14–32, which stressed the need for cooperative enterprise in the West. That the frontier fostered inventiveness has also been disputed, particularly in Fred A. Shannon, "An Appraisal of Walter Prescott Webb's *The Great Plains,*" *Critiques of Research in the Social Science:* vol. 3 (New York, 1940). Allan G. Bogue, "Pioneer Farmers and Innovation," *Iowa Journal of History,* vol. 56 (January 1958), pp. 1–36 presents evidence to show the opposite, using case studies of an Iowa county. Daniel J. Elazar, *The American Partnership* (Chicago,

1962) reveals the manner in which westward expansion fostered a nationalistic spirit in the United States. That several historical writers, and notably Turner, have helped engender an intense nationalism by their own writings is the theme of David W. Noble, *Historians against History: The Frontier Thesis and the National Covenant in American Historical Writing* (Minneapolis, 1966).

In addition to Everett S. Lee and David M. Potter, whose works are represented in this book, other students have advanced alternative explanations of the distinct features of the American character. George W. Pierson joins with Lee in making a case for mobility; the most searching of his several articles on the subject are "The M-Factor in American History," *American Quarterly*, vol. 14 (Summer 1962), pp. 275–289, and "A Restless Temper . . .", *American Historical Review*, vol. 69 (July 1964), pp. 969–989. Louis Hartz, *The Liberal Tradition in America* (New York, 1955) traces many American characteristics to the lack of a feudal background.

Modern students of the frontier recognize that it was only one of a variety of forces operating to mold the American people; they realize also that its influence was relatively slight and that inherited traits and practices persisted to a large degree. This is the theme of the excellent article by Earl Pomeroy that appears in this volume. An attempt to reinterpret the frontier thesis with proper recognition to these additional factors is Ray A. Billington, *America's Frontier Heritage* (New York, 1966). What is often viewed as an extension of the Turner thesis is the stimulating volume by Walter Prescott Webb, *The Great Frontier* (Boston, 1952), which deals with the effect of the end of European expansion on the world of the future.